CW00692421

Ginger bread

1/2 ℔ Treacle 1/2 ℔ Sugar 9 oz Butter
Ginger to your taste — a few Cloves & a
little lemon skin — Rub the butter in
as much flour as will make the paste
stiff adding flour till it is so when
you knead it — when the butter &
treacle are stiff with cold set them
within the air of the fire to soften
in warm weather this is not
necessary —

Blacking

4 oz Ivory black 2 oz course sugar
mixed well with a quart of vinegar — add carefully 1/2 oz Oil of
vitriol stirring very well on
a stick in a deep earthenware vessel
last of all add two large spoons
of sweet oil —

To preserve fruit of any kind
gather the fruit when dry & to
a pint of fruit take 1/4 ℔ Loaf
Sugar (or fine soft will do) put
the fruit & Sugar into jars or

wide necked Bottles a layer of
sugar and a layer of fruit —
Tye the jars down with wet
bladders — set them in a pan of
cold water on the fire — let it boil
full half an hour — or untill you
think the fruit is enough done —
Take it off the fire and let the jars
stand in it until it is stone cold
then cover the bladders with double
paper — Apples, Pears, Seberian Crabs
may be done in this way —

Custard Pudding

A pint of good milk (better with
some cream) 4 Eggs — a small
spoonful of Flour — boil it 40 minutes
then take it out of the water, and
cut it up ½ an hour at least —
put it in the boiling water again
for from 5 to 10 minutes —

Yeast

Boil 1 oz of hops about 10 minutes
in 6 quarts of water — Strain it and
mix it immediately with 2 lb of
flour and a tablespoonful of sugar

Cooking and Dining
with the Wordsworths

FRONTISPIECE - The ladies who cooked for William Wordsworth; his wife Mary, sister Dorothy, and (below) sister-in-law Sara Hutchinson.

Cooking and Dining
with
The Wordsworths
From Dove Cottage to Rydal Mount

Peter Brears

Excellent Press
Ludlow

First published in 2011 by Excellent Press
9 Lower Raven Lane
Ludlow SY8 1 BL

ISBN 1 900318 43 1
ISBN 978 1 900 318 43 3 (*paperback*)

ISBN 1 900318 47 4
ISBN 978 1 900 318 47 1 (*cased*)

*The author has donated his royalties from sales of this book
to the Wordsworth Trust and Dove Cottage*

Printed in Malta

CONTENTS

PREFACE
by
Jeff Cowton MBE
Curator, The Wordsworth Trust

As curator of the Wordsworth Trust's collections, I have been privileged to work with Peter in the preparation of this book. His enthusiasm and knowledge have brought alive a subject hitherto unexplored in such depth; his research adds greatly to our understanding of life in Dove Cottage during the Wordsworths' residence from 1799-1808.

Dove Cottage, at the heart of the English Lake District, is the house most closely associated with Wordsworth's major writing. He chose it as his home when he was 29 years old, looking to dedicate his life to poetry amongst his 'native mountains'. His devoted sister, Dorothy, shared his home and was to live with him for the remainder of her life. Between 1800 and 1803 she kept a journal, she wrote, 'for the pleasure it will give William', and this records beautifully their life together, the places they visited and the people they met. Wordsworth married Mary Hutchinson in 1802, and three of their five children were born in Dove Cottage. It became a family home, often noisy and crowded, and led Dorothy to write at the age of 34: 'I think these years have been the very happiest of my life.' It was where Wordsworth wrote his most popular lines, 'I wandered lonely as a cloud', as well as the first full-length version of the great poem of his life, *The Prelude*.

The Wordsworths shared this hamlet of Town End with only three neighbouring dwellings; the road passing through its centre was a main thoroughfare, described by Dorothy in 1805 as 'the highway of the Tourists', busy enough even then for her to complain to a friend about its noise! In her journal she describes passers-by knocking and begging at her door. Life in Grasmere could be idyllic: daily walks, rowing and fishing on the lake, creating and enjoying their orchard and garden (their 'little domestic slip of mountain'), reading books and having friends call in or to stay (including key figures of the day, such as Samuel Taylor Coleridge and Sir Walter Scott). But as Wordsworth himself wrote: 'Yet 'tis not to enjoy that we exist...something must be done.' That something was the writing of poetry 'On Man, on Nature and on Human Life', subjects with which we are equally concerned today. The research that Peter has done, and the books that he has published help us better understand life in the modest white cottage that was the background to the writing of some of the greatest poetry in the English language.

The cottage, and most of the hamlet, is now owned and cared for by the Wordsworth Trust, established in 1891. Its purpose is to preserve Dove Cottage and its environs, and its growing collection of manuscripts, books and art, and to use them to promote a greater appreciation of the life and work of Wordsworth and the writers and artists of what we now call the 'Romantic period'. We are fortunate that their lives are extremely well documented through their poetry and prose, and that the Jerwood Centre at the Wordsworth Trust has such a rich reserve of archive material. Amongst the many thousands of manuscripts are the recipe books described in such detail in this book. Peter has used these materials to provide the context for the food that they ate, and at the same time given colour (and taste!) to what we already know.

Peter has drawn upon two principal manuscripts for his work: the first is a notebook shared by Dorothy and Mary, which came to the Trust in the late 1970s, as part of a collection that was discovered in Carlisle and which included the now famous 'love letters' written between William and Mary in 1810 and 1812. The second notebook was compiled by Joanna Hutchinson, Mary Wordsworth's sister, and came to the Trust in 1981, having descended through the family. A third source is still in private hands, and has been kindly loaned to the Trust by a great-great-great-grand-daughter of Samuel Taylor Coleridge: it contains recipes recorded by the Fricker family, two of whom (Sara and Edith) married the poets Coleridge and Robert Southey. These two poets and their families joined Wordsworth in the Lake District, settling in Keswick, 13 miles north of Dove Cottage. We are very grateful to Rosemary E. Coleridge Middleton for her generosity in lending these beautiful manuscripts.

It has been such a great pleasure to get to know Peter during his time in Grasmere. Memorably, he gave a talk on this subject and provided tablefuls of delicious food prepared using the recipes and methods described in the book. The lecture was fascinating, and the samples a treat. I recommend you not only devour his words and knowledge, but put the recipes to the test as well. You won't be disappointed.

ACKNOWLEDGEMENTS

I would like to thank Esther C.B.Rutter for first asking me to lecture at Dove Cottage. Following this, Jeff Cowton, Curator at the Wordsworth Trust, informed me of the Wordsworth, Hutchinson and Fricker manuscript cookery books in the Trust's extensive archives. Since I had already undertaken studies of the traditional foods of the Lake District, and re-created the kitchen of the poet's childhood home at Wordsworth House, Cockermouth, I fully appreciated their unique interest. I cannot thank Mr Cowton and all his staff at Dove Cottage enough for all their help while I was working there. Both he and Mrs P. Woof, President of the Wordsworth Trust, also read through my initial text, making valuable suggestions.

I would also like to express my warmest thanks to Susan Houghton for all her considerable assistance, my publisher, David Burnett, for his care in putting the book through the press, and Miriam Macgregor for her artwork, seen on the front cover. A special word of thanks to Valerie Thomas for her scrupulous care in preparing the manuscript for press, and for many valuable suggestions. Finally, I would like to record my appreciation of the Red Lion and Lamb Inn, Grasmere, a warm and welcoming retreat from the torrential rains, deep snows and biting frosts during the harsh winter of 2009-10.

Peter Brears
Leeds, 2010

INTRODUCTION

Throughout the English-speaking world, the works of the Romantic poets of rural late Georgian Britain are recognised as some of the greatest of all literary achievements. William Wordsworth and his vision of the Lake Counties are inseparable from this movement, continuing to give the greatest pleasure to his readers, in addition to providing a seemingly endless source of study for scholars. For over a hundred and fifty years there has been a continuous stream of books on Wordsworth, his family and friends, some being labours of love developing the very highest standards of research, writing, and editorship. There is, however, one fascinating aspect of his life that has received very little attention and on which there is a considerable body of valuable information.

In the extensive collections of the Wordsworth Trust at Dove Cottage, William's first home in Grasmere, are four early nineteenth century recipe books, the first written by his wife Mary, the second by her sister Joanna, the third by Martha Fricker, sister-in-law to both Samuel Taylor Coleridge and Robert Southey, and a fourth from the Fricker family. In all, they provide over 125 recipes used in their households. They have never been subject to any previous detailed study, and so are presented here for the first time. One of the primary purposes of this book is therefore to enable readers to cook and taste the same dishes as William Wordsworth and his circle, the necessary instructions being drawn from the original manuscript sources. A second, but more interesting and enlightening aim, is to combine the information in the recipe books with the vast wealth of other material and manuscript sources, including Dove Cottage itself, Dorothy Wordsworth's great Grasmere Journals of 1800-1803, and the correspondence of William, Dorothy and Mary Wordsworth, and of Sara Hutchinson, together with other contemporary documentation. It purposely avoids most of the creative and biographical aspects of their lives, since these have already been subject to considerable study, but instead concentrates on all matters culinary. In taking this approach I hope to review and reveal much additional information on the homelife of the Wordsworths, not so much as poets and writers, but as members of a somewhat irregularly organised household, growing ever more conventional with the acquisition of larger houses and higher social status.

The ladies responsible for preparing the poet's food and organising his domestic life came from the professional and minor gentry classes. In their earlier years they had experienced similar circumstances, but with significant differences, all of which influenced their approach to food and the levels of skill they developed in their kitchens. We must therefore start by introducing each of them in turn, following their lives up to the point of William and Mary Wordsworth's marriage towards the end of 1802, and describing their recipe books. Only then can we move on to explore the practical aspects of life at Dove Cottage and the increasing reliance on servants to undertake the cookery in the family's later houses.

In each succeeding chapter, the type of food eaten by the Wordsworths is considered in turn. Having drawn together all the relevant references from the family's extensive writings, they go on to provide transcripts of the original recipes, followed by instructions for making them today, if still practicable, which most are. For the convenience of today's cooks the modernised instructions are for reduced quantities, since today's households are far smaller than those for whom most of the originals were prepared. Where the Wordsworth recipe books do not contain details of a particular dish, its recipe has been drawn from an associated source such as one of the contemporary local cookery manuscripts, Coleridge's notebooks, or regionally significant publications like Mrs. Raffald's *The Experienced English Housekeeper*. Working directly from the original recipes can prove highly problematic, for their methods may be unclear, the quantities unsuitable for modern use, or the oven temperatures and cooking times missing. In addition, they frequently assume a level of knowledge that we may lack today, being written more as aides-mémoires for personal use, rather than as comprehensive instructions for strangers. For this reason each recipe is accompanied by an authentic yet modernised version, with measurements in pounds, ounces, pints and tablespoons, as well as in grams and litres. All measurements of volume are for level, rather than heaped quantities, while all eggs are of 'medium' size. As for temperatures, these are given in degrees Centigrade, Fahrenheit and Gas mark for a conventional oven. If using a fan-assisted oven these should be reduced accordingly. No attempt has been made to provide healthy alternatives for the authentic ingredients. Traditional recipes abound in saturated fats etc., which can lead to health problems, since our life-styles no longer burn them off. Similarly more people today require vegetarian or vegan options. It is therefore left to personal preference to use low-fat or vegetarian alternatives for the cream, butter, suet etc. quoted in the recipes. For every other ingredient, however, it is best to use local organic produce, such as Herdwick lamb or mutton, beef, pork, poultry, fish and game. As for flour, any good plain wheat variety may be used, but certainly not wholemeal, which the Wordsworths would never have bought, it then being considered decidedly third-rate.

In today's England, there is an enormous demand for ethnic or 'fusion' foods from everywhere but England. This is largely due to the economic problems and periods of rationing which marked the first seventy years of the twentieth century here. In ordinary homes, in country houses, inns, hotels and restaurants, the great national tradition of excellent cooking and baking suffered enormously, many of our finest dishes and highest culinary skills being largely forgotten. Instead of being revived when circumstances allowed, they were replaced by a hotch-potch of foreign dishes from France, Spain, Italy, Greece, India, China and even America. In contrast, the recipes reproduced in the following pages illustrate few international influences, being essentially those of the Georgian north-country middle-class. Their tea, coffee, rum, sugar, spices and other exotic ingredients were certainly shipped in from around the expanding Empire, but perhaps the only imported recipe in this collection is that for an excellent lemon pickle, based on those from India. As for the rest, they are purely English, using basic methods to convert local produce into a range of satisfying dishes, all of which are well worth reviving for everyday modern use. Some may prove rather surprising: those hostesses who boast of their pannacotta, for instance, will discover that it is just an inferior-flavoured English blancmange which in its delicious native version still makes by far the best accompaniment for Lythe Valley damsons, preserved to Mary Wordsworth's own recipe. Certainly all the recipes carefully noted down by Mary, her sister Joanna, and their Fricker contemporaries should not only be read, but also tried, in order to gain a fuller knowledge of the lives and lifestyles of all those who made up their illustrious households.

Chapter One

THE WORDSWORTHS
& THEIR RECIPES

Throughout his working life, from 1794 to 1850, William Wordsworth was fortunate in having a succession of practical ladies who provided him with every domestic service he could ever require, leaving him free to concentrate on his work.

His sister Dorothy acted as his secretary and copyist. She was also responsible for running his household – a responsibility she largely relinquished to William's wife, Mary, after his marriage in 1802. Dorothy and Mary had been close friends since childhood, and the household duties were often shared out even more widely during frequent long visits and residences from Mary's sisters, Joanna and Sara Hutchinson. This chapter explores the backgrounds of these key figures in William's life and their effect on the domestic arrangements at the houses where they lived in and around Grasmere: Town End (later renamed Dove Cottage), Allan Bank, Grasmere Rectory and finally Rydal Mount, a large house overlooking the vale of Rydal.

William himself had enjoyed an idyllic childhood at Cockermouth, where his elder brother Richard and younger siblings Dorothy, John and Christopher were under the tender care of their mother Ann. Unfortunately this period of great happiness and security came to an end on the death of his mother in March 1778, when William was just seven years old. This close family was now scattered, the last links with Cockermouth being cut when their father died in 1783.

From 1779 to 1787 William attended the grammar school at Hawkshead, lodging in the home of Ann Tyson, who acted almost as a foster-mother to several schoolboys. 'She gave all she could of that sort of simple, unpretentious rustic affection and discipline that seems like the very quality of the countryside distilled into human terms.'[1] Working on a fixed budget, she provided basic and nourishing food though William recalled that it was not over-plentiful:

No delicate viands sapp'd our bodily strength;
More than we wish'd we knew the blessing then
Of vigorous hunger, for our daily meals
Were frugal, Sabine fare! And then, exclude

A little weekly stipend, and we lived,
Through three divisions of the quarter'd year
In pennyless poverty.[2]

When he moved on to St. John's College, Cambridge, in 1787, William
found himself in rooms in the first court, where

Right underneath the College kitchens made
A humming sound, less tuneable than bees,
But hardly less industrious; with shrill notes
Of sharp command and scolding intermix'd.[3]

Meals were constantly available in hall, but, especially as a 'fresher',

... The weeks went roundly on,
With invitations, suppers, wine, and fruit.
Smooth housekeeping within, and all without
Liberal and suiting Gentleman's array! [4]

The years following his departure from Cambridge in 1790 were
spent in travelling through France and Switzerland, touring Wales
and Wiltshire, and spending long periods in London. In January 1794
he was able to achieve a long-planned reunion with his sister Dorothy,
spending six weeks with her with friends, Elizabeth and William
Rawson, in Halifax, before travelling on to Keswick, walking the last
thirty three miles from Kendal via Ambleside and Grasmere. It was
in Keswick, at Windy Brow, that Dorothy first exercised her skills as
housekeeper for William. 'We please ourselves in calculating from our
present expences for how very small a sum we could live. We find our
own food, our breakfast and supper are of milk and our dinner chiefly
of potatoes and we drink no tea.'[5]

Dorothy's training for this lifelong role had probably started in
the family home at Cockermouth, where she had been born in 1771.
Here her father, John Wordsworth, was the attorney and 'law-agent'
to Sir James Lowther, the chief landowner and political magnate of
the district. To enable him to fulfil his professional and social duties,
Sir James housed John Wordsworth in one of the finest properties
in town. Standing at the west end of the main street, with a large
walled garden extending down to the River Derwent, it had been
built by Richard Bird around 1690, and then extensively remodelled
to the highest standards around 1745 for John Lucock, Sheriff of

Fig 1. The kitchen at Wordsworth House, Cockermouth, was fully equipped with stewing stove, roasting range, oven and boiler. Here the Wordsworth children would have seen their mother Ann prepare fine dinners for her husband's guests, until her early death in 1778, when they were dispersed to school and distant relatives.

Cumberland. Its elegantly panelled entrance hall, office, dining room and first-floor drawing room were ideal for conducting the business and entertainment required to promote Sir James's extensive interests. Most of the other rooms were severely utilitarian, being used to house the family and a few servants. However, the house was provided with all the necessary offices. The semi-basement contained a dairy, a wine and ale cellar and a larder, while the kitchen had a large charcoal stewing stove, a roasting range, oven, and built-in dresser. Dorothy would have seen all of these in full operation in her early childhood, but had little chance to absorb any of the skills practised there before her mother died when she was six years old.

Unable to look after all his young family, John sent Dorothy to live with his mother's cousins, Elizabeth and William Threlkeld of Halifax. This extended household, already occupied by Elizabeth's orphaned nieces and nephews, provided both happy memories and lifelong friends. But all was to change in May, 1787, when Dorothy, who had been orphaned at John's death in December 1783, joined her maternal grandparents and her brothers, for the summer in Penrith. The young Wordsworths had had a miserable time here, being subject to constant indignities and insults, particularly from the servants. This time, however, it did bring a renewal of friendships made years earlier at the local dame school with the Hutchinson children, who were also orphaned and now in the care of their Penrith grandfather. Following their brief reunion, Dorothy went to live at the rectory of her uncle, William Cookson, at Forncett in Norfolk, staying with him until reunited with her brother William, first at Halifax and then at Windy Brow in 1794. A year later William and Dorothy moved on together to Racedown Lodge in Dorset and to Alfoxden House in Somerset in 1797. They visited the Wye Valley, and then embarked on a study-expedition to Germany, finally returning to England in May 1799. After a few months with the Hutchinsons, now at Sockburn-on-Tees in the south of County Durham, Dorothy joined William at Town End, Grasmere, setting up home in the former Dove and Olive Bough Inn on 20th December 1799, now Dove Cottage.

In her Grasmere journals, which run from May to December 1800 and October 1801 to January 1803, Dorothy recorded many of the cooking operations she carried out there. This considerable body of archival evidence has led a number of writers to assume that she was a great cook, running the Wordsworth's domestic affairs for the rest of her life. However, a closer reading of the journals and letters shows that this was not the case. Throughout much of her early life she had lived in relatively small households which employed only the basic standards of everyday cookery. There is no evidence to suggest that she ever had any opportunity of being trained to the levels of culinary skill usual amongst most contemporary middle and upper-class families, in which ability in domestic management was seen as an essential requisite for making a good marriage. Record offices and private family archives contain probably thousands of manuscript books of recipes collected by well-to-do young women, some being continued throughout their adult lives. They all demonstrate a high degree of practical competence, including a knowledge of both materials and techniques which it would be difficult to achieve even today.

As the journal entries show, Dorothy was perfectly capable of baking, brewing, and of producing basic nourishing meals composed of potatoes, vegetables, plainly-cooked meats and fish, and pies. When she had no other help but Old Molly Fisher, this is what she produced. However, when anything more was required, she found herself in difficulties. She was unable to raise the oven to its correct temperatures in July 1800, so that the pies could not be baked, while in May 1802, still susceptible to bad advice, she managed to produce a cake 'as black as a genuine child of the coal-hole' and completely inedible.[6] In August 1800 she was so uncertain of the proportion of sugar to fruit necessary when preserving, elementary knowledge to anyone with basic cookery skills, that she had to try three different batches and record the results.[7] It is interesting to note that the journals of 1800 – 1802 only mention cake-making when one of the Hutchinson sisters was a guest at Dove Cottage, except for one seed cake for her friend Mr Simpson.[8] Another telling comment on Dorothy's cookery at this period comes from a letter which William wrote to Mary in May 1812, after meeting Mr Carr, Solicitor to the Excise, in London. In it, he recalled 'the very bad dinner which he had the misfortune of receiving, or rather dearest Dorothy and I had the vexation of giving him in our Little Cottage at Grasmere, before you and I, my Love, were married.'[9] After Mary's permanent entry into the household as William's wife in October 1802, there were no more culinary disasters. Then, as Dorothy recorded in her journal: 'We made cakes' on 16th October, Mary was baking on 23rd October and 8th December, while on 24th December we find 'Mary... in the parlour below attending to the baking of cakes', and on 16th January 1803 'we [are] going to... make Gingerbread ourselves.'[10]

Mary seems to have been rather too busy cooking, child-rearing and managing the family's finances to have had time to record her own daily activities. For this reason, it has frequently been presumed that she did very little beyond the incidental activities that Dorothy noted in her journal, but there is substantial evidence that this was not the case. In reality she and Dorothy carried out their domestic responsibilities in tandem, assisted for long periods by Sara and Joanna Hutchinson, and demonstrated a remarkably good-humoured and mutually rewarding relationship - united in providing their beloved William with every opportunity to pursue his amazing creativity.

The Hutchinson family had been brought up in Penrith, where their father John was a tobacconist. There were four brothers, John, Henry, Thomas (Tom) and George, as well as three sisters, Mary, Sara, and Joanna, who had attended the same local dame school as the young Wordsworths. Their father died in 1785, being buried in Penrith on 2nd April. Sara then went to live with her cousin Margaret Robinson who had married James Patrick, a Scottish pedlar now settled in Kendal. All the other children moved in with their maternal aunt Elizabeth Monkhouse, under the watchful eye of their grandfather John Monkhouse, post-master of Penrith. William Wordsworth later described him as 'the most gentlemanly man, both in looks and manner, that I ever knew in Penrith.'[11] In addition to his town property, he owned a small estate at Sebergham, a few miles south of Carlisle, where the children spent very enjoyable holidays. His wife was Margaret Richardson of Nunwick Hall on the Eden, a member of one of the most considerable county families in the district. The Hutchinson children were therefore being brought up in much happier, more prosperous and more gentlemanly circumstances than their Wordsworth contemporaries. In addition, since they all could expect either to inherit estates or marry into good families, their guardians appear to have provided them with the necessary practical and social skills. In contrast the Wordsworth boys needed a grammar school education and professional training to counteract the uncertainty of their futures caused by Sir James's arbitrary decision to withhold massive sums owed to their deceased father. It is probable that there was a strong tradition of good housekeeping in Mary's family, for in the year of her birth Arthur Young, the great agriculturalist, published a description of hospitality he had received at Penrith, at Mr Monkhouse's New George inn. This, he found, was 'Exceedingly good, reasonable, and very civil. The dinner was roast beef, apple pudding, potatoes, cellery, potted trout and sturgeon. 1s a head.'[12]

When Dorothy came to live with her Cookson grandparents in Penrith in 1787, and William started to spend his vacations from Cambridge there in 1788 and 1789, their friendship with the Hutchinsons began to centre around the eldest sister, Mary, who would eventually would become established as Dorothy's lifelong friend and as William's wife. In the meantime, however, Tom Hutchinson had inherited his great-uncle's farm of Sockburn Hall, a peninsular of County Durham, where the Tees looped into Yorkshire just east of Darlington. The elder Thomas Hutchinson had been one of the great livestock breeders of the eighteenth century, his Sockburn sheep and shorthorn cattle enjoying a very high reputation in agricultural circles. As Dorothy recorded in 1795, the house was:

> ...built by their uncle, who left them the furniture and eighteen hundred pounds, which with what they had makes them very comfortable. It is an excellent house, not at all like a farm-house, and they seem to have none of the trouble which I used to think must make farmers always in

a bustle, for they have very little corn and only two cows. It is a grazing estate, and most delightfully pleasant, washed nearly round with the Tees (a noble river) and stocked with sheep and lambs which look very pretty, and to me give it a very interesting appearance.[13]

This now became the family home, with brother Tom at its head, and Mary as his housekeeper, assisted by her younger sisters. George, the youngest brother, also lived here, the eldest brother John being in business in Stockton-on-Tees, and the second brother Henry then at sea. Having no permanent home of their own, William and Dorothy Wordsworth spent considerable periods here as friends and house-guests, including a continuous seven months from May to December, 1799. Even after the Wordsworths moved into Dove Cottage, they continued to keep in close touch with the Hutchinsons through letters and visits.

In 1802 Tom, Mary and Joanna moved from Sockburn to Gallow Hill near Scarborough, while George took a farm at Bishop Middleton near Bishop Auckland in County Durham. Thus it was to Gallow Hill that William and Dorothy returned after their tour of Germany, arriving in the middle of the corn harvest at the end of September 1802. A few days later, on 4th October, William and Mary were married at Brompton Parish Church, returning only briefly to the house to have breakfast and board the chaise hired to take the three back to the marital home in Grasmere. As Dorothy recorded in her journal, 'Mary was much agitated when she parted from her Brothers and her Sisters and her home.'[14] This was to be expected, for even though she had already stayed at Dove Cottage for several months, and knew it well, she would now have to establish herself as wife and principal housekeeper of an already established household, and one not as extensive or so well provided for as the one she was leaving. In effect, she had been the chatelaine of a relatively well-to-do establishment for eleven years, fully responsible for its domestic management, except while making visits elsewhere, when her sister Joanna had taken over.

Compared to Dorothy, Mary was very competent and experienced in all things domestic. This is illustrated by her surviving recipe book. It takes the form of a vellum-bound pocket-book with marbled end-papers, measuring some six and a half by four and a half inches (16·5 x 11·5cm).[15] There are only eighteen recipes, but these include instructions for making blancmange, jaunemange, artificial ginger, and Portuguese vegetable soup, all of which might be expected in a rather more prosperous and pretentious house than Dove Cottage. It also contains remedies such as tonics, footbaths, eye waters and horse plasters. There is little internal evidence for its date. At the end of the recipes, and therefore most probably written some time after they were in use, are several pages of miscellaneous accounts, most being in Mary's hand and dated between 1815 and 1820, when the family had settled at Rydal Mount. Among them are entries such as:

'Rydal Mount up to Jan 7 1817	9 3 9'
'4 Days house work	4 -'
'Tom's Clothes [the Wordsworth's second son]	
2yd and half of calico at 1/8 per yard	[3 4]
2 and a half of checks	1 4
pair of shoes	7 -
2 yards of check for shirt	- -'
'1820 2 Baskets	3 -
Received of Mrs [?] for candlestick	1 3
2 flower pots (self)	6
2 Candlesticks	6
Match Boxes	8'
'butter sold	
Mary young 2pd paid	2
Nanny Patty 3pd	3
Mary Young 1pd	
Nanny Patty 1pd'	

There is also a list in Dorothy's hand of what she had paid for 'J. Hutchinson', presumably Joanna, including accounts with various ladies, £2. 4s for tartan, 11s for rugs, and £6. 6s 'For Taffy to Boy', along with £3.13s 2d for corn and 2s 8d for a blacksmith. However, the most moving of all is a separate entry for August 1816 'Tombstone £3. 4s -.' This would be to mark the grave of William and Mary's six-year-old son Thomas, who died in 1812. Later Mary was to complain that it took William 'years to produce those 6 single lines upon the stone at the head of the earthly remains of our own dear Boy'.[16] With the exception of these accounts, the recipes in this book are far too few in number to represent the working collection of a full-time housewife and cook. They are essentially Mary's working copies, made for occasional use - but copies of what? Three of them, those for rice, a pickle for hams, and the Portuguese vegetable soup, are actually in the handwriting of her sister Joanna. As for the remainder, the best clue comes from her recipe for

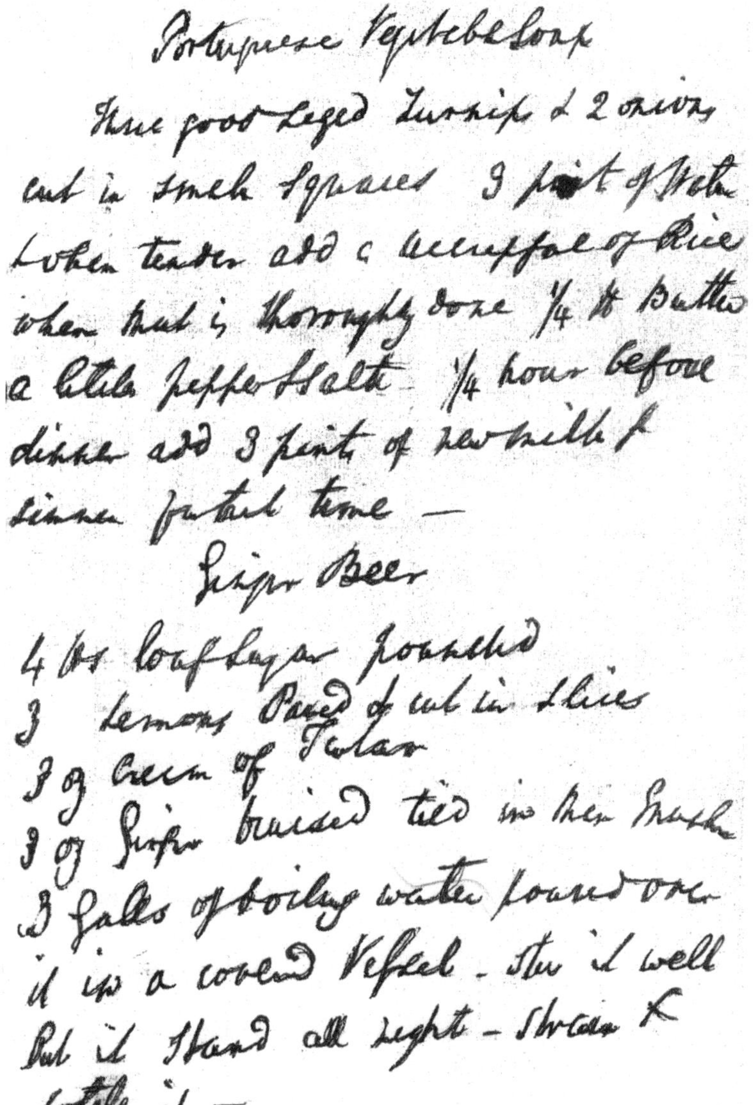

Portuguese Vegtebel Soup

Three good Leged Turnips & 2 onions
cut in small Squares 3 pint of Water
& when tender add a teacupfull of Rice
when that is thoroughly done ¼ lb Butter
a little pepper & Salt - ¼ hour before
dinner add 3 pints of new milk &
dinner put at time —

Ginger Beer

4 lbs loaf Sugar pownded
3 Lemons Pared & cut in slices
3 oz Cream of Tartar
3 oz Ginger bruised tied in thin Mushn
3 Galls of boiling water poured over
it in a coverd Vessel - Stir it well
let it Stand all night - Strean &
bottle it —

Fig 2. A page from Mary Wordsworth's recipe book, showing an example of her handwriting below, and that of her sister Joanna Hutchinson above.

gooseberry wine. This was either copied from one in the second recipe book in the Wordsworth Trust's collection, that of her sister Joanna, or from a common source, such as that of the unidentified original 'Mrs Kes...', or from an earlier Hutchinson family recipe book. Whatever the case, we may be sure that, as in most polite Georgian families, all the sisters would have developed similar repertoires of recipes during the long years they had spent together at Penrith and Sockburn. In essence, it is reasonable to assume that Mary would be familiar with the practical use of all the recipes in Joanna's book. Joanna herself never visited Grasmere before Mary's marriage, but already shared a close friendship with the Wordsworths, having given Dorothy a fine shawl in April 1802.[17] She first stayed at Dove Cottage in the autumn of 1803, providing company for Mary and baby John while William and Dorothy went off on a tour of Scotland with William's friend and fellow poet Samuel Taylor Coleridge. She was later to spend considerable periods in the Wordsworth household.

Joanna's recipe book, commenced in 1816 or earlier, and later inscribed 'Miss Joanna Hutchinson, Hindwell Hall, July 14, 1821', is fully worthy of that title. It is a card-covered book measuring some seven and three-quarters by four and a half inches (19·5 x 11·5cm), its thirty-six pages being packed with seventy-four closely-written recipes.[18] It has main courses of chicken, calf's head, pig, chicken, and game, eight hot and cold puddings, ten cakes, eight pickles and preserves, and thirteen wines and drinks, as well as a good selection of household and medicinal recipes. It is interesting to speculate whether William really did carry the odour of mothballs with him, having shaved with its home-made wash-balls containing camphor, or if his wife and sisters were scented with the rosewater and almond oil used in its cold-cream.

The third recipe book, loaned to the Trust, belonged to Martha Fricker. She had very little contact with the Wordsworths, spending most of her life in the south of England. The fourth daughter of the Fricker family of Bristol, she had been born in the family home on Redcliffe Hill in 1777. Her three elder sisters had been caught up in the idealistic plans for Pantisocracy, a scheme for setting up Utopian communities in which all were equal and all ruled. In the mid 1790s, when three of the girls were in their early twenties, they had each married one of its charismatic leaders, Sara, the eldest, marrying Samuel Taylor Coleridge, Mary, the second, marrying Robert Lovell, and Edith, the third, marrying Robert Southey. The Pantisocratic life they envisaged marked a giant leap from the conventions of the day. As

Coleridge described, they would:

> "let the married Women do only what is absolutely convenient and customary for pregnant Women or nurses - Let the Husbands do all the Rest & Washing with a Machine and cleaning the House. One Hour's addition to our daily Labor" [19]

He even noted down recipes for stew, ginger wine etc. ready for use as part of his husbandly duties.[20] Even when married and responsible for his first son Hartley, Coleridge still believed that he could live by working:

> "very hard as Cook, Butler, Scullion, Shoe-cleaner, occasional Nurse, Gardener, Hind, Pig-protector, Chaplain, Secretary, Poet, Reviewer, and omnibotherum shilling-scavenger in other words, I shall keep no Servant, and will cultivate my Land-acre, and my wise-acres, as well as I can." [21]

Needless to say, when these high intentions came up against the harsh realities of life, they rapidly crumbled. If the married Fricker girls really believed that their husbands would undertake every domestic chore and maintain them in the manner to which they aspired, they were to be sadly disappointed.

William and Dorothy Wordsworth had first met Coleridge during a five-week visit to Bristol in August-September 1795, immediately preceding Coleridge's marriage to Sara Fricker, which took place at the magnificent church of St.Mary, Redcliffe, on 4th October. Their friendship and working relationship then flourished through their time at Racedown and Alfoxden, at Sockburn, in Germany and into the years at Dove Cottage. After returning to the West Country in May, 1800, Coleridge came back to the Wordsworths at the end of June, now accompanied by Sara, baby Hartley, and all his books, in preparation for moving into Greta Hall, Keswick, on 24th July. Eventually his brother-in-law Robert Southey brought his family up to share the Hall, along with Robert Lovell's widow and young son. This, in effect, meant that its domestic affairs were entirely in the hands of the three re-united Fricker sisters, Sara, Mary and Edith. As for Martha, she had been courted by George Burnett, another Pantisocrat, but had rejected him and remained single in the south of England. She hardly ever travelled to Keswick to see her sisters, but did spend some time at Greta Hall in the summer of 1812.[22]

Martha Fricker's recipe book measures some six by four inches (15 x 10cm), is vellum-bound, and inscribed 'Martha Fricker January 1st 1814' inside its cover.[23] Its contents are chiefly medical remedies and instructions for whitening marble, removing ink stains, or making Indian glue, etc. There are culinary recipes too, for typical middle-class dishes of the period, from curing hams and making broth, to making cakes and puddings.

The fourth recipe book, on loan to the Wordsworth Trust, is also associated with the Fricker family, but it does not bear the name of any individual.[24] It measures eight and a quarter by five inches (21 x 12·5cm), with twenty-six pages containing twenty-seven recipes. Its main significance is that, unlike the previous books, it concentrates on cookery for a family used to giving high-class dinners. There are no egg and bacon pies, no boiled puddings. Its recipes are largely for fashionable confectionery, the kind of dishes intended to grace dining rooms and drawing rooms in the fine Bath-stone merchant houses of prosperous Bristol. Here are the lightest of sponge cakes, rich iced plum cakes, delicate creams and jellies, and even crème brulée. Given these aspirations and this standard of domestic training, the Fricker sisters were brought up to a more leisured way of life than the Wordsworths and the Hutchinsons. It is not surprising that Dorothy, while respecting Sara Coleridge's 'several great merits', found her to be 'a sad fiddle fuddler', taking three and a half hours just to dress herself and her two young children, only then coming down to her family's Sunday dinner, obviously prepared by others.[25]

It is particularly fortunate that the recipe books of Mary Wordsworth and Joanna Hutchinson have survived, since they provide instructions for making over ninety of the dishes probably served in the Wordsworth household. However, as with most records of this kind, they present an essentially incomplete account of most of the food actually cooked and eaten on a daily basis. No-one needed an aide-mémoire for making porridge, boiling or roasting meat, or cooking vegetables. Again, it is truly remarkable that so much of the Wordsworths' correspondence has not only survived, but has also been published in full, to provide a wealth of information regarding even these seemingly most insignificant of details. By combining such essential sources with close observation of their first marital home, Dove Cottage, it is now possible to reconstruct their domestic life with a high degree of accuracy.

Chapter Two

AT HOME IN GRASMERE

What kind of household did Mary Wordsworth enter as a new bride in October 1802? As her husband recorded, their house was a former inn called The Dove and Olive Bough which had:

> Offered a greeting of good ale
> To all who entered Grasmere Vale ...
> There, where the Dove and Olive-Bough
> Once hung, a Poet harbours now,
> A simple water-drinking bard.[1]

In a later letter to the Rev. Francis Wrangham, Wordsworth described it as 'our tiny cottage', where there was only 'very homely fare, no wine and even little beer'.[2] Over the following years, this concept of 'plain living and high thinking' was maintained and perhaps even developed with Eleanor Rawnsley describing how they had lived on nothing but bread, porridge, potatoes and milk, tea being far too expensive, and how they considered themselves fortunate to have a well of water in the garden, so that they could at least quench their thirsts.[3] Similar passages have effectively created a myth of William and Dorothy's 'noble poverty' at Dove Cottage. The only poverty they encountered was that which they observed in others, the homeless beggars wandering by their door, or the local families working every hour of the day to place even the most basic level of subsistence food on their tables. Being provided with a totally unearned income to support private grammar school education, years at Cambridge University and continental tours, and also to maintain a sequence of houses and a decidedly middle-class lifestyle, is to be considered prosperous, even wealthy, by both Georgian and modern standards. Plain living should never be confused with real poverty.

Similarly Dove Cottage could only be described as 'tiny' by someone like William who was used to life in mansions which today would be valued at around a million pounds or more. The real tiny cottages of the Lake counties were very basic one or two-roomed structures with walls of either beaten clay or local stone, roofed with thatch or slate, their only fire being lit in open smoke-hoods at one end.⁴ Despite its relatively modern title of 'cottage', in 1800 'Town End' as it was then known was one of the best houses in Grasmere. It was two-storeyed, well-built with six main rooms, all but one having their own fireplace fitted with an iron grate. The culinary activities were centred on three ground-floor rooms.

In common with most middle-class families, the Wordsworths used two kitchens. The back kitchen, half-buried in the rising ground to the rear of the house, served as a combined pantry/ scullery/ washhouse/ and general kitchen for food preparation. To one side, it had a larder, with a channel of fresh water running beneath its slate floor to ensure that it always remained ideally cool. Here, on its shelves and its slate-slab-topped 'stone' or bench, all raw and cooked foods should have been stored, as in a modern domestic refrigerator. However, the unconventional Wordsworths apparently chose to use this room as their peatroom, giving them an indoor supply of domestic fuel. It is probable that they stored their ale barrels here too, since all the other rooms would have been far too warm for keeping ale in good condition. This meant that the back kitchen had also to serve as a pantry for the storage of food, its left-hand wall having a large cupboard furnished with shelves to hold all the family's dry stores - everything from rice, tapioca and dried fruits, to jams and preserves. The back kitchen/pantry had a slate-flagged floor and a low, beamed ceiling with wrought iron hooks at its centre. These were carefully positioned for hanging hams and pieces of bacon up in the slightly warm draughts drawn towards the fire, keeping them in ideal conditions and well away from people's heads, since the main worktable would be directly below. It would be from here that Coleridge probably cut himself a rasher of bacon to accompany the peas he had gathered from the garden in early August 1802, making a meal for himself while the Wordsworths were away in Calais.⁵ The present fireplace is fitted with a mid-nineteenth-century cast iron oven to the right, a soot-door just below it, and the brass knobs above to operate a scraper, which prevented soot accumulating on its top, behind the faceplate. The wrought iron firebox of the grate extends to the left, terminating in a rectangular cast iron boiler with a brass tap from which to draw off supplies of hot water. All of these features date from long after the Wordsworth's departure, however, and in their place we should imagine a typical Georgian open fireplace, a single, large rectangular opening extending from the floor up to a long horizontal mantle-beam. Since coal would be burnt here, a wrought iron grate would have been set in the middle of the back wall, ready to roast or toast anything placed before it. Above, bridging across the chimney opening, there would be a high-level randle-balk or beam, from which cooking pots could be hung over the fire, by means of adjustable iron reckon-hooks. The oven would have taken the form of a large masonry-domed chamber, its rectangular door opening at about waist height into the side of the fireplace, so that its smoke would be readily carried away up the chimney. If there was a sink, it would have closely resembled the lead-lined example still to be found here, but it is equally likely that the function of a sink was then performed by a freestanding coopered tub mounted on a low stool-like stand.

The front kitchen, or kitchen parlour, the room that Dorothy referred to as 'the Kitchen' or 'the Parlour', was the main room at the front of the ground floor.[6] As the 'bar parlour' of the Dove and Olive Bough, it had a hard-wearing slate-flagged floor and walls clad in panelling most atypical of traditional cottages. The present whitewashed plaster ceiling is a later addition, for in the Wordsworth's day it was still open to the floorboards, so that all conversations held here could be easily overheard by all in the room above.[7] This was the main living room, a combination of entrance hall, dining room, parlour and kitchen. The panelling around the present inserted fireplace shows how it was originally much larger, housing a cooking grate to complement that in the back kitchen. In 1800 Dorothy described how 'after the dishes are washed up we let [this] kitchen fire go out, and we never light it till it is time to dress the dinner.'[8] By its side casual visitors were entertained as they told their stories. Here too Dorothy continued her writing while keeping a watchful eye on the roasting mutton, the family also reading around it, and sometimes taking their teas and dinners.[9] This was the bustling, cramped room in which William would:

> ... sit without emotion, hope or aim,
> By my half-kitchen, my half-parlour fire,
> And listen to the flapping of the flame,
> Or kettle whispering its faint undersong.[10]

The adjacent parlour was used as a bedroom, initially by Dorothy, then by William from the summer of 1802, and by both William and Mary after their marriage. Having a door into the front kitchen, it was ideally placed for serving breakfasts or suppers to William, on those occasions when he took these meals in bed.

Two short flights of stairs and a half-landing led up to the first floor, where the room over the kitchen/parlour was used as the family's more private sitting room. Breakfasts and teas were taken here, as well as dinners. On Christmas Day, 1805, for example, Old Molly and John Fisher were to leave the kitchen 'when dinner is ready ... to come upstairs and partake' in this family sitting room.[11] Before the houses were built across the road, it enjoyed splendid open views across Grasmere to Silver How and the encircling fells. This was William's refuge when foul weather kept him indoors, Dorothy describing how it:

> ...often compelled my brother to [remain in] the sitting room when in a milder season he would have composed in the open air, indeed I cannot but admire the fortitude and wonder at the success with which he has laboured in that one room, common to all the family, to all visitors, and where the children frequently played beside him.[12]

The room over William's bedroom was used as a lodging room for their numerous visiting friends and relations, while that over the larder/peat room was improved to provide a separate bedroom for Dorothy.[13] The last room upstairs, that over the back kitchen/pantry, served as a lumber room.

As for the Wordsworths, it can be confirmed that, as Eleanor Rawnsley stated, they ate bread, porridge, potatoes and milk. However, she was totally incorrect in claiming that they consumed nothing else. Meat, including beef steaks, veal and mutton as well as bacon was probably delivered by the butcher's man from Ambleside.[14] There were also geese and turkeys in the winter months, as well as occasional gifts of game, such as partridges from their friend Lady Beaumont.[15] Freshwater fish for the table were the product of local fishing expeditions. Between May and August 1800, for example, William and his brother John caught three pike and three bass in Grasmere, and three pike in Wythburnwater (now under Thirlmere).[16] The pike weighed up to 4¾ and 7½lb. For these their methods included both rod and line, and setting hooks baited with small dead fish on floated lines.[17] They also fished in Rydalwater and in Langdale, but their catches there were not recorded.

Most of their fruit and vegetables were either home-grown, or received as presents from friends. Peas, for example, were sown around early April, tended both by John and Molly Fisher, by Dorothy, provided with sticks, some made by William, in June, and harvested in baskets from late June through to the end of August, some being kept as seeds for the following year.[18] Considered a delicacy, some fresh green peas were given to their neighbour Mrs Simpson, and by a chaise returning to Keswick, to the Coleridges.[19] Scarlet or French beans came a little later, being sown in early June, tied and nailed up by Dorothy in early August, and harvested from July to the end of September.[20] In 1800 she described Dove Cottage being 'covered all over with green leaves and scarlet flowers, for we have trained scarlet beans upon threads, which are not only exceedingly beautiful but very useful, as their produce is immense.'[21] Given the basic details given in her journal, it is possible to reconstruct the seasonable availability of vegetables from the garden:

Beans, French[22]	late July – September
Beans, Kidney[23]	July – August
Broccoli[24]	October – March
Carrots[25]	October – March
Onions[26]	October – March
Peas[27]	June – September
Potatoes[28]	Most of year
Radishes[29]	May – September
Spinach[30]	October – June
Turnips[31]	October – March

The garden was also used to grow both culinary and medicinal herbs such as the 'lemon thyme and several other plants' that Dorothy planted by moonlight after a visit to the Simpsons, or the wild thyme gathered on a ramble on the hillside above the house.[32] Apple and pear trees in the orchard provided both fresh fruit and ingredients for pies and tarts, and there were rhubarb, gooseberries and strawberries to be had too.

William probably acquired both a taste for honey and the knowledge of how to collect it while at school in Hawkshead, where, returning for his vacation from Cambridge, he laid himself 'down to any casual feast of wild wood-honey' in the surrounding countryside. Ann Tyson had previously purchased honey for William, to satisfy his schoolboy yearnings for this sweet treat.[33] Peggy Ashburner gave Dorothy 'some honey – with a thousand thanks', in November 1801, in return for a gift of hot roast goose. Dorothy then decided to 'set her right', explaining that there was neither expectation nor need to repay such presents from a friend.[34] There might have been a hive in use in the garden by 1802, however, the bees buzzing around it

Fig 3. John Fisher's bee-stand at Sykeside, just opposite Dove Cottage.

in late January, and John Fisher sodding 'about the Bee-stand' at the end of April.[35] Bee-stands are shown in W.J. Blacklock's painting of a farmstead in Little Langdale of 1850, small four-legged tables, each of them supporting its traditional domed lipwork straw skep protected by what appears to be a white linen cover.[36] The garden at Sykeside, the Fishers' cottage just opposite Dove Cottage, still retains a bee-stand much more substantially constructed in stone. It has an open-fronted cupboard-like recess for the hives, and is protected by a sloping roof above. The hives at Town End would have provided the Wordsworths with sufficient honey to spread on their tea-time toast, as well as wax for polishing the furniture, making cold-cream, and similar domestic preparations.

As for the drinks taken by this 'simple water-drinking bard' and his sister, they included home-brewed beer, wine, coffee, and quantities of very expensive tea. There was milk, too, but not in large quantities, as the family did not acquire its own cow until after leaving Dove Cottage.

Fuel to cook the food, as well as to keep warm, came in three different forms. Dry fallen branches and sticks were collected during the course of frequent local walks, some being formed into faggots to heat the oven, and others being chopped into logs by William to burn as fuel.[37] Peat was also burned here, Dorothy recording the raising of the former peat-room roof to create her new bedroom in June 1805.[38]

It was cut from local peat-beds in late spring: 'The people were graving [digging] peats under Nadel Fell' in mid May 1802, which were laid out in strips to dry, and then carted back to the homesteads at midsummer, when the Wordsworths saw Colwith 'wild and interesting, from the Peat carts and peat gatherers.'[39] Some of the small farmers in Grasmere then sold part of their stock of dried peats to those unable to obtain their supplies in any other way, George and Sarah Green of Easedale earning much-needed money in this way.[40] This is how Dove Cottage peats would have been obtained. When looking for a new house in 1810, the Wordsworths had considered Bouth, six miles south of Kendal, one of its positive factors being that it enjoyed peat-digging rights, the expense of collecting them being only £8, a much cheaper way of heating a house than using coal.[41]

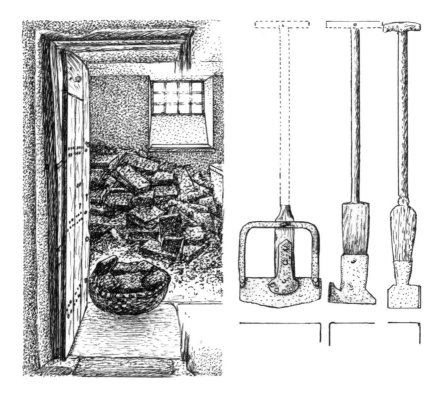

Fig 4. The Dove Cottage peat-house was in this small room off the back kitchen/pantry. In the Lake District peats were cut out of the moors and fells either in broad slabs, as with the spade from Wasdale Head near Shap (left) or in narrow strips, as with the spades from Hawkshead (middle) and Lowick, High Furness (right).

There were no coalfields near Grasmere, but coal was extensively burned in the more urban areas, Keswick being supplied from the great West Cumberland mines around Whitehaven, and Kendal from Ingleton etc., full access to the Wigan pits not being possible until the completion of the Lancaster Canal in 1819. Between 16th May and 1st November 1800, Thomas Ashburner, the local carrier and their close neighbour, delivered ten loads of coal to Dove Cottage, that is about one load per month.[42] They usually came from Kendal, only being carted more expensively from Keswick in times of scarcity.[43]

Having supplied Dove Cottage, the nature of the daily routine of its inhabitants can now be considered. In most households the needs to take the maximum advantage of daylight working hours, of feeding staff, and foddering livestock, together with other practical considerations, made it imperative to maintain a regular domestic timetable. One of the distinguishing characteristics of Dorothy's housekeeping, however, was that there was hardly a trace of any routine of any kind. To provide William with the maximum freedom to work as he wished, spending as much time as possible composing or travelling in the open air, every trace of a timetable was abandoned. Most houses would devote a particular day of the week to a particular purpose, such as cleaning, laundry, baking, etc., but as Dorothy's journal shows, this was not the case at Dove Cottage. Baking might happen not only on any weekday, but also on a Sunday, the established day of rest throughout the rest of the community, when best clothes were worn, the Bible read, and as little domestic work as possible carried out.[44]

It was generally accepted that the efficiency of a household could be judged by the regularity of its mealtimes. Coleridge's notebooks contain the following routine:

> Six o'clock, light the fires, Clean out the Kitchen, Put on the Tea Kettle. Clean the Insides of the Boiling Pot, Shoes &c. ...
> Eight o'clock. Tea things &c, put out [for breakfast] & after cleared up ...
> One o'clock – spit the meat
> Two o'clock – Vegetables &c ...
> Three o'clock – Dinner
> Half past three – 10 minutes for cleaning Dishes [45]

In contrast, under Dorothy's management, breakfast might be served at any time from around 8am to 1pm, dinner from around noon to 5pm, tea up to around 7.30pm, and supper some time later.[46] Such flexibility might suit the poetic mind, but is hardly ideal for promoting good digestion. It is therefore no surprise to find that the journal makes frequent references to stomach upsets. Dorothy must have been well aware of the situation, explaining to her close friend from her Halifax days, Jane Marshall, that 'I [can] [?not] tell you how we pass [the time] because our employ[ments are] not very various yet they are irregular.'[47]

Having spent some eleven years as mistress of a working farm, Mary Wordsworth must have found such a deliberately disorganised house extremely difficult to comprehend when she took up her role as William's wife. It is interesting to speculate why Dorothy's journal and letters makes little or no reference to her personal involvement in the subsequent changes. It is quite certain, however, that Mary's need to maintain a well-organised household was effectively adopted by Dorothy, who by early 1804 was explaining to Lady Beaumont that 'it is an affair of great consequence to us that we should be well served and that all things in our little establishment should be regularly organised.'[48] How different from 1800 – 1802! Mary's efficiency as a domestic manager greatly impressed all who saw her carrying out this role. When Canon Rawnsley interviewed those who remembered her, they recalled how she was:

> ...terb'le particular in her accounts, never allowed you an inch in the butching book.
> A close-fisted woman, that's what she was.
> ...and she was a manasher an 'aw', an kepp t'accounts. For ye kna he nivver knew aboot sec things, nayder what he had or what he spent.
> Mrs Wudsworth, she was a downright clever woman, as kep' accounts and was a reg'lar manasher. He never know'd, bless ye, what he hed, not what he was wuth, not whether there was owt to eat in t'house, nivver.
> Why, she was a manasher, niver a studier, but for a' that there's nea doot he and she was truly companionable, and they wer terr'ble fond o' yan anudder. But Dorothy hed t'wits on 'em boath.[49]

Since Mary's death in January 1859, successive writers have seen Dorothy as the chatelaine of Dove Cottage and the Wordsworths' later homes in Grasmere and Rydal, relegating Mary's contribution to the shadows. Nothing could be more unjust and untrue. Providing all essential domestic services for her family, and its numerous long and short-term guests, and fulfilling William's particular needs, were full-time and challenging tasks. Mary appears to have executed them with commendable efficiency and skill. Unlike her husband and sister-in-law, she apparently lacked both the free time and probably the inclination to record her experiences for posterity, but her contribution to their comfort, security and well-being should never be under-estimated.

To run their growing household, both Dorothy and Mary relied on practical help from servants and female relations. On moving into Dove Cottage, Dorothy found that the sister of their neighbour John Fisher had aired it by lighting small coal fires over the previous days. This was Mary, better known to the Wordsworths as 'Old Molly'. As William told Coleridge in a letter written on Christmas Eve, 1799:

> We do not think it will be necessary for us to keep a servant. We have agreed to give a woman [Old Molly], who lives in one of the adjoining cottages two shillings a week for attending two or three hours a day to light the fire wash dishes etc., etc. In addition to this she is to have her victuals every Saturday when she will be employed in scouring, and to have her victuals likewise on other days if we should have visitors and she is wanted more than usual. We could have had this attendance for eighteen pence a week but we added the sixpence for the sake of the poor woman, who is made happy by it. [50]

By September 1800 Molly's duties had been expanded to include gardening and laundry, Dorothy describing her as:

> ...an old woman 60 years of age whom we took partly out of charity and partly for convenience. She was very ignorant, very foolish, and very difficult to teach, so that I almost despaired of her, but the goodness of her disposition and the great convenience we should find if my perseverance was at last successful induced me to go on. She has now learned to do every thing for us mechanically, except those parts of cooking in which the hands are much employed, for instance she prepares and boils the vege[tab]les and watch the meat when it is made ready for roasting, looks to

the oven etc ... she has washed the linen of all our visitors except the family of the Coleridges during that month. [We have] great washes about once in 5 weeks, and she washes towels, stockings, waistcoats, petticoats etc. once a week, such as do not require much ironing. This she does so quietly, in a place apart from the house, and we know so little about it as makes it very comfortable. She sleeps at home ... and in winter it is a considerable saving of fire that her home is so near, for after the dishes are washed up we let the kitchen fire go out, and we never light it till it is time to dress the dinner, and she employs herself at home. She is much attached to us, and good as ever was a human being.[51]

Mary got on well with old Molly from her visit in the autumn of 1801, being provided with such information, irrelevant to her marriage, as 'Ye may say what ye will but there's nothing like a gay auld man for behaving weel to a young wife. Ye may laugh but the wind blows no favour – and where there's no love there's no favour.'[52] Her help in most aspects of domestic work was considerable, Dorothy finding herself extremely 'tired with making beds, cooking etc' when Molly fell ill in June 1802.[53] She was soon back to her duties, however, including helping Dorothy and sitting with Mrs Simpson during her convalescence.[54] In early May, 1804, following her sister-in-law's death, Molly had to take on the full responsibility for John Fisher's housekeeping.[55] The friendship with the Wordsworths continued as close as ever, however, young John Wordsworth cramming himself with her cream porridge and cakes, and Dorothy accepting her presents of home-made butter, for example. It only ended with Molly's death at Grasmere on 3rd June, 1808.[56]

From May 1804 her place was taken by a fifteen-year-old servant from the Vale of St. John.[57] In the Lakes it was customary for all male and female servants to attend the hiring fairs held in the market squares each Whitsuntide and Michaelmas, there to be inspected and interviewed by potential employers, who would hire them for the following six months. It would have been at such a fair that someone to whom Dorothy referred as their 'Old servant' (probably Mary Dawson), found fresh employment in May 1806, leaving only a twelve-year-old girl to serve them. Dorothy hoped to hire someone else by the end of June, but female labour was fast disappearing into the cotton mills, where the wages were far higher.[58] By March 1808 the family was being served by two servants and little Sally Green, the daughter of the Easedale couple who had recently been found dead in the snows towards Langdale. The pressure of housing William, Mary, Dorothy, Sara Hutchinson, the four Wordsworth children and three servants in the confined space of Dove Cottage was now causing severe problems, but these were largely alleviated by the removal to the much larger Allan Bank, Grasmere, towards the end of May.[59]

In addition to servants, the unmarried Hutchinson sisters also provided domestic help during their visits. Sara, the youngest, first stayed here in November and December 1800, sharing 'a great baking' with Dorothy, and returning again in December-January 1802-3.[60] From the following year she acted as Tom Hutchinson's housekeeper at Park House near the foot of Ullswater, then joined the Wordsworths from October 1806 on their winter visit to Coleorton in Leicestershire, after which she became their virtually permanent companion.[61] In June 1803, Mary had given birth to the Wordsworth's first child, John. When he was just two months old, William, Dorothy and Coleridge deserted her for a six-week tour of Scotland. Fortunately Joanna Hutchinson, author of the recipe book, was able to move to Dove Cottage in order to provide the necessary support. She stayed on for a whole year before moving in with Tom at Park House, but retained strong links with her Grasmere relations.[62] In June 1806, for example, Dorothy recorded how;

> 'Johnny likes being with his Aunt Joanna very much and she says he is a good Boy; he is quite at home among horses and cows.'[63]

Descriptions of some of the meals cooked at Dove Cottage were given by Dorothy in her journal, and it is probable that details of those taken in the family's later houses were very similar. As one indoor servant remembered:

> Nay, nay, Wudsworth was a man as was fond of a good dinner at times, if you could get him to it, that was't job; not but what he was a very temperate man i' all things, vara, but they was all on 'em mean livers, and in a plain way. It was poddish for t' breakfast, and a bit o' mutton to t' dinner, and poddish at night, with a bit of cheese happen to end up wi'...Mrs. Wudsworth would say "Ring

the bell" but he wouldn't stir, bless ye, "Goa and see what he's doing," she'd say, an we wad goa up to study door and hear him a mumbling and bumming through it. "Dinner's ready, sir," I'd ca' out, but he'd goa mumbling on like a deaf man, ya see. And sometimes Mrs. Wudsworth 'ud say, "Goa and brek a bottle, or let a dish fall just outside in passage." Eh dear, that maistly wad bring him out, wad that. It was nobbut that as wad, howivver. For ye kna' he was a vera careful man, and he couldn't do with brecking t' china.[64]

In taking porridge for breakfast, the Wordsworths were following the north-country practice of most poor and many middle-class families.[65] Made by sprinkling coarse oatmeal into a pan of boiling water while stirring vigorously, and continuing to stir as it slowly thickened, it was hot, satisfying and nutritious. The usual way of eating it was to hold a mug of milk in the left hand, dipping in each spoonful of porridge before raising it to the lips, but there is no evidence to confirm that this method was followed at Dove Cottage. Broth might also be taken at breakfast, as a lighter and more savoury alternative. In March 1802, for example, Dorothy made William 'his Basin of Broth ... and little plate of Bread and butter [as] he wrote a Poem to a Butterfly!'[66] Bacon and eggs were certainly available, but probably appeared at breakfast only when requested by visitors such as Coleridge.

Dinner, the main meal of the day, was again plain but nutritious in the 'meat and two veg' tradition which continued in England to the late twentieth century. Potatoes and seasonal vegetables provided the usual accompaniment to joints of legs of mutton, William's favourite meat, these being roasted, and probably boiled too.[67] Other meats included mutton chops, beefsteaks, pork and, rarely, hare and partridge, some of which would be roasted before the fire, broiled on an iron grill, or put into a dish, covered with pastry, and baked as pies.[68] Poultry appeared only rarely: goose when at its best in late autumn, turkey on Christmas Day, and fish only when caught locally by the family or its friends.[69] For dessert, there might be pies made from home-grown apples, pears, gooseberries, etc., or local damsons, either fresh or preserved.[70] The family also enjoyed richer dinners from time to time: for example, one served in September 1820 included hare soup, Stickle Tarn trout and venison.[71] They enjoyed similar fare when dining out, Mary describing to Dora the 'turbot, then a leg of most tempting looking mutton, Pidgeon Pye, Lemon Pudding and open sweetmeat tart, Dessert etc.' taken with young William in Carlisle.[72] Such dinners were sometimes replaced by much lighter snacks if appetites were low, Dorothy recording a dinner composed solely of 'a bason of Broth ... which seems to settle well with me', or another of two boiled eggs and two apple tarts.[73]

The best description of teatime at Dove Cottage comes from Thomas De Quincey:

> This, with the Wordsworths, under the simple rustic system of habits which they cherished then, and for twenty years after, was the most delightful meal of the day ... because it was prolonged into a meal of leisure and conversation ...[74]

In addition to the all-essential pot of tea, their favourite tea-time treat was fresh, hot buttered toast, William later recalling one afternoon when:

> My sister and I were in the habit of having the tea-kettle in our little sitting room and we toasted the bread ourselves ... one morning when we had a young prig of a Scotch lawyer to breakfast with us, my dear sister, with her usual simplicity, put the toasting fork, with a slice of bread, into the hands of this Edinborough genius. Our little bookcase stood on one side of the fire. To prevent loss of time he took down a book and fell to reading, to the neglect of the toast, which was burned to a cinder. Many a time we have laughed at this circumstance, and other cottage simplicities of that day.[75]

De Quincey recalled how William conducted himself when both reading and toast were being enjoyed simultaneously:

> Wordsworth took down the volume [as] tea was proceeding ... Dry toast required butter; butter required knives; and knives lay on the table; but sad it was for the purity of [the book's uncut] pages, that every knife bore upon its blade testimonies of the service it had rendered. Did that stop Wordsworth? Did that cause him to call for another knife? No at all: he
> > Look'd at the knife that caused his pain,
> > And look'd and sigh'd and sigh'd again

and then, after this momentary tribute of regret, he tore his way into the heart of the volume with this knife, that left its greasy honours upon every page, and are they not there to this day?[76]

William appears to have been something of a connoisseur in the matter of buttered toast, observing at an inn breakfast at Baldock that it was 'for all the world as if it had been soaked in hot water'.[77] John Pippingill's depiction of William seated at just such a coaching inn table shows rolls, rather than toast, being kept hot on a plate placed over a deep basin of hot water.[78] Other teatime specialities would include home-made preserves and honey to accompany the toast, cakes and gingerbread.[79]

As in most households supper was a relatively light meal, probably based on the cold meat left over from dinner, cheese and bread and butter and pickles. Its informality is illustrated by the supper-dishes mentioned in Dorothy's journal, these including cold mutton, eggs, broth, or pasty-pudding, while a later servant's account of the family describes them supping on basins of new milk and a loaf of bread.[80]

More elaborate meals would certainly have been cooked and served when entertaining guests, or when celebrating the major annual festivals. On Christmas Day 1805, for example, young John Wordsworth was 'all alive at the thought of two plum-puddings which are now rumbling in the Pot, and a Sirloin of Beef that is smoking at the Fire', their alternative Christmas roast being the turkey.[81]

Within a few months of arriving at Grasmere, the Wordsworths had discovered the delights of rowing out to the island in its lake, there to light a fire and enjoy a picnic. It was here that they entertained the Coleridges just before they moved into Greta Hall, Dorothy's journal recording how they all 'drank tea at the island. The weather was very delightful ...'[82] Coleridge's account conveys a much fuller and more enthusiastic image of the event:

We drank tea the night I left Grasmere, on the island in that lovely lake; our kettle swung over the fire hanging from the branch of a fir-tree, and I lay and saw the woods and mountains, and lake all trembling, and as it were idealised through the subtle smoke which rose up from the clear red embers of the fir-apples, which we had collected: afterwards, we made a glorious bonfire on the margin, by some elder bushes, where twigs heaved and sobbed at the uprushing column of smoke – and the image of that bonfire, and of us that danced round it – ruddy laughing faces in the twilight – the image of this in a lake as smooth as that sea, to whose waves the Son of God had said Peace! May God and all his Sons love you as I do.[83]

Such delightful picnics were repeated over the years, Dorothy noting 'the Ashes of the fire and the smoky stones we had left after boiling our kettle upon the Island' in 1803.[84] As with all the best- planned of Lakeland's outdoor events, the region's unpredictable weather could cause real problems. In August 1808 'Nineteen [of] us were to have [had] a Picnic upon Grasmere Island ...and all were caught in a thunder shower, and all wet to the skin on the way to the lake side. The feast was Mr Crump's, our [Allan Bank] Landlord ...We dined at the Inn.'[85] After removing to Rydal Mount, picnics were taken by Rydalwater, using two nice new boats; 'we take our Tea bathing & load with fuel at [the island] I stand and dr[ink] Tea on the opposite shore for the Islands

Fig 5. Dinners taken at Robert Newton's inn next to Grasmere churchyard cost just 10d (4p) each.

are so full of wood that there is no safety in making a fire upon them ... It is beautiful beyond all description,' wrote Sara Hutchinson.[86] Picnics continued to play an important part in every summer's social entertainment over the following years, as in September 1826 when 'we had a huge picnic party into Easedale', or in late August 1827, when 'we also had a picnic meeting under Raven Crag lying by the margins of Wytheburn – the families of Greta Hall and Rydal Mount, with other vagrants, making a party of about 30 – merry group we formed round a gypsey fire upon the rocky point that juts from the shore, on the opposite side of the lake from the high road.'[87]

Outdoor meals were as much a necessity as a pleasure when taken on the Wordsworth's long walks and rides across the region. The most convenient food for such journeys appears to have been sandwiches: William's sandwich tin, with its hinged lid, still survives in the Wordsworth Museum at Grasmere. Their contents were either cold meat or potted meat, sometimes supplemented with a piece of sweet cake or apple.[88] Inns and ale houses provided further refreshment. At its best, this could represent excellent quality and value, as at Seathwaite in the Duddon Valley, where they enjoyed 'Tea, Supper and Breakfast – Excellent cream and delicious bread and butter – broiled Char fresh out of the Tarn to supper. – Tea 1s – Supper 1s – Breakfast 1s – Horse 1s – ale 6d – Total 4s 6d!'[89] At another inn near Ullswater, 'We had a good supper; ham, veal, cutlets, preserved plums, ale, rum and water, dry beds and a decent breakfast. We paid 7/– one shilling too much.' At another at Kirk Ulpha they enjoyed tea, boiled ham and eggs.[90] Usually their chosen travellers' fare was rather simpler, however, such as the tea and ale, bread and cheese, etc. eaten heartily at the King's Head, Thirlspot, beneath his sign:

> J STANDLEY lives here & sells good Ale
> Come in & drink before it grows Stale -
> John Succeeded his Father PETER
> But ith' old mans time 'twas never better [91]

Alternatively there might be a first course of porridge followed by Christmas pies, as eaten in a public house in December 1801.[92]

It is interesting to follow the quite separate diet prepared for the Wordsworth children while in their infancy at Dove Cottage. John, or 'Johnny', the eldest, was born on 18th June 1803, the christening at Grasmere Church on 15th July being followed by 'christening cake, tea and coffee' at the cottage.[93] Mary appears to have suckled him from the start, but by the time he was five months old he was only taking milk and 'what he sucks out of a piece of meat or a crust of Bread while we are at our meals. He is generally so quiet at these times that it is quite a trial [i.e. problem] to have him at table with us ...We are going to get him a tall chair that he may sit up at Table by himself, for in a little while it will not be very convenient to eat with him upon our knees, he stretches out for everything.' [94] In February 1804 he was inoculated with cow-pox, to prevent him catching the deadly and disfiguring smallpox, but it failed to take, and had to be repeated a little later. [95] On 8th April Dorothy noted that he was taken from his mother's breast: 'At first he was silent & low spirited not very fretful. In two or three Days he began to ask for food very impatiently ... NB on Thursday 14th April he first got upon his feet by himself, with the aid of a stool ... William wagered a guinea with me that he would walk in a fortnight.' [96] By the time he was eighteen months old he had already been fed on broth too, but since it was thought to inflame a skin problem on his forehead, it was decided that he should be fed solely on bread and milk, quite a common regime for babies at this period. [97] One of his favourite dishes now became the rich 'Cream porridge which he sucked in most greedily at Molly's', but he was soon taking his share of his parents' meals. [98]

After the Wordsworths' move to Allan Bank in May 1808, their domestic circumstances changed considerably. This was a gentleman's villa, offering more and better rooms for both family accommodation and domestic services. It also offered sufficient land for Mary and Sara to utilise their farmhouse experience in keeping a cow to provide milk, cream and butter, as well as pigs for bacon. [99] The house incorporated numerous severe practical faults, however, including wet cellars and chimneys that perpetually smoked. It was so bad that they had to cook in the study 'and even heated water there to wash dishes, for the Boiler in the Back kitchen could not be heated, much less the kitchen fire endured ... we have been more than a week together at different times without a kitchen fire ... Dishes are washed, and no sooner set in the pantry than they are covered with smoke ... the smarting of the eyes etc., etc. you may guess at.' [100] Sara confirmed this appalling situation:

> 'Not a chimney will draw the smoke, and one day we could not have a fire except in the Study; and then you could not see each other. In the rest of the rooms the fire was actually blown out of the Grates.' [101]

Martha Fricker's recipe book offered this solution:

Cure for Smoky Chimneys

A wire-gauze front to be fitted over the [fire] place, of about twenty two wires to the inch. The effect of which is said to be instantaneous. [102]

The Wordsworths had no knowledge of this method, and it would probably have been ineffective against their hurricane-like down-draughts. These and other difficulties continued throughout their occupancy, despite the efforts of workmen to rebuild chimneys, improve the dining room etc.[103] In terms of domestic management, one of the major changes was the employment of a full-time cook/cow-keeper, 'a very good servant', to prepare the meals including dinner at 3pm.[104]

In early June 1811, they removed from Allan Bank to Grasmere Rectory, a house which had two parlours, four bedrooms for the family and one for the servant, a store-room, cellar, dairy, pantry, and 'a decent small kitchen'. The Rector, Mr. Jackson, agreed to add a library and a new back kitchen.[105] There were also a kitchen garden, space enough for breeding cows and pigs, and fields in which to grow hay for the cattle and potatoes for the house.106 Dorothy described the

'hay-making which was a throng [busy] time, for both our Servants were obliged to go out constantly, therefore Mary and I had to make beds, cook and attend the children. I made a large seed-cake ... and was employed in making preserves and picking gooseberries.' [107]

On May Day, 1813, the Wordsworths moved again, this time to Rydal Mount, which was to become their home for the rest of their lives. It was originally a farmhouse called Keens, but a fashionable front suite had been added in about 1760, with elegant rooms offering open views across the vale of Rydal on to the fells opposite. It was a gentleman's house, and was furnished accordingly, the dining room being provided with an expensive Turkey carpet, Wedgwood tableware and fine glass decanters.[108] 'You stare, and the simplicity of the dear Town End Cottage comes before your eyes,' wrote Dorothy, 'and you are tempted to say "are they changed, are they setting up for fine folk? for making parties – giving Dinners etc? No, no." ' [109] In fact, despite

Fig 6. Rydal Mount, drawn by Dora Wordsworth around 1830. The family moved in on Mayday, 1813, and remained here for the rest of their lives.

their wish to retain their simplicity of lifestyle, they were in reality setting up a conventional well-to-do household, complete with a butler; one that had nobility to dinner, and held balls. 'Were I to give you a list of the folks we have had & our consequent engagements,' wrote Sara, 'it would make a list as long as that of Crosthwaite Museum [in Keswick].' 'The dining room looks so comfortable, warm & genteel you would be delighted with it.'[110] Mary also described a ball for which 'the dining room was ridded of all superflous furniture and dressed out in Christmas's gayest garb – the festoons of glittering Holly with its red berries etc. etc., was carried round the walls – the floor chalked in great taste.'[111] Chalking the floors of ballrooms was a highly skilled task, usually undertaken by a professional, who used coloured chalks to give the boards the appearance of an elegant parterre, or a richly inlaid marble floor. They were a transient luxury however, as William had described in *Personal Talk* written back at Dove Cottage:

> These all wear out of me, like Forms with chalk
> Painted on rich men's floors, for one feast-night.

To carry out such entertainments effectively, it was essential to have the services of a good cook, but at the end of April 1814, Dorothy found that:

> Unfortunately we happen for the last year to have had the worst cook in England - but Mary Dawson is coming to live with us at Whitsuntide (whom you remember was our servant at Town End) and Sara and I intend to give her unlimited commission to cook all sorts of nice things for Mary [who] in these little things would be far more easily ruled by a servant than by us.[112]

Mary Dawson was later replaced by a cook called Jane, who apparently proved unsatisfactory, for in September 1819, following 'our unhappy cook's misery, we have got a delightful young woman in her place, who is always cheerful, tidy and good humoured, and in the management of her fires, that never-ending plague when Jane was here, she is exactly the opposite of Jane, and cooks well with less fuel than any servant we ever had.'[113] Within a year, however, there were renewed problems, Sara describing how she was awaiting the return of Mary Bill at Martinmas, since the current cook at Rydal Mount, one Mary Anne, was 'as smooth & polite as possible, but I do not like such smoothness if I were to say black was white to my face she would agree to it. Cross-tempered maids shall always have my favor in preference & I should be sorry if this smooth-faced, & insincere creature were here to greet you. I have hired a cook from Keswick, who I hope will do well, 'tho I have not seen her.'[114] Throughout their years at Rydal Mount the family always employed a full-time cook, only coming into the kitchen either to give orders or to undertake the preparation of a particular dish.[115] Their last cook was a typically practical and down-to-earth lady, who took no pleasure from the beauties of nature. When asked if she had seen a particularly wonderful sunset, she replied, 'No & I'm a tidy cook, I know, and, they say, a decentish body for a landlady, and sic-like, but I nivver bodder nowt aboot sunsets or them sort of things, they r'e nowt ataw i' my line.'[116]

Back at Dove Cottage, between Mary Wordsworth's arrival as a new bride in 1802 and the family's departure to Allan Bank in 1808, she and Dorothy had undertaken all the cookery required for their family and its numerous guests. Along with her sisters Joanna and Sara, she had previously been provided with an excellent training in culinary skills, and had had many years experience as housekeeper to a gentleman-farmer's establishment. The survival of Mary's recipe book, and that of her sister Joanna, is extremely fortunate, since it provides an invaluable insight into the dishes that would have been cooked at their Grasmere and Rydal homes. In the following Chapters all the recipes are reproduced and explained, along with those of Martha Fricker, and others from contemporary sources, for dishes mentioned by the Wordsworths, but for which no manuscript recipes survive. Together they provide a unique insight into the domestic life of one of the English language's greatest poets.

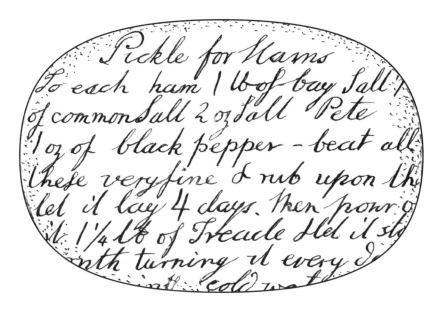

Pickle for Hams
To each ham 1 lb of bay Salt 1
of common Salt 2 oz Salt Pete
1 oz of black pepper – beat all
these very fine & rub upon th[e]
let it lay 4 days. Then pour o[n]
[.] 1¼ lb of Treacle & let it st[and]
[mo]nth turning it every d[ay]
[... i]nt[o] cold wat[er]

Chapter Three

OF MAIN COURSES

The foods served at dinners and suppers in late Georgian Grasmere varied enormously in their quality and quantity, according to the wealth and resources of each individual or family. Those who took their meals at Robert Newton's, the inn just to the north of the churchyard, might pay only tenpence for:

> Roast pike, stuffed; a boiled fowl; Veal cutlets and Ham; Beans and bacon; Cabbage; Peas and Potatoes; Anchovy sauce; Parsley and butter [sauce]; Plain butter [white sauce]; Wheat bread and oat cake; Three cups of preserved gooseberries, with a bowl of cream in the centre.[1]

This was by no means exceptional travellers' fare, for at the King's Arms in Kendal Christopher Fenton would provide:

> A boiled fowl and sauce, roast partridge, potted charr, cold ham, tarts, and three or four foreign sweetmeats 8d a head. [or] cold ham, tarts, potted charr, anchovies, butter and cheese 6d a head.[2]

In contrast, families such as the Greens of Easedale were so poor that they had to barter their bridles etc. for a few potatoes. These, with a little oatmeal, a few pieces of lean dried mutton, and a daily quart of milk from their cow, were all that they could afford even in the coldest months of winter.[3] The Wordsworths' close neighbours, the Ashburners, may have been better off, but even they had to subsist on a mean diet of 'oatbread, milk and porridge by a fireside'.[4] In a letter to her lifelong friend Catherine Clarkson, Dorothy confirmed that she would rather survive on such poor fare than go into the banishment of emigration forced upon some of her contemporaries. However, the food they enjoyed at Dove Cottage was certainly superior to this, even if not of the quantity served in the local inns.

Various references show that their kitchen fire was equipped with pots and pans for stewing and boiling, a gridiron for broiling or grilling, some means of roasting meat before the fire, and most probably a frying pan too. These, in addition to an oven in the back kitchen/pantry, enabled them to prepare their food in every usual way. To make the broths sometimes served for breakfasts or suppers, and as a first course at dinner, for example, they would have used a covered boiling pot to simmer a joint of meat. Its stock could then be thickened with barley in the local tradition or with dumplings, such as Dorothy once made for John Marshall, proprietor of the world's largest flax mill, and husband to Dorothy's friend Jane Pollard.[5] Mutton broth appears to have been a favourite, even being served to Sir Francis and Lady Vane, the Wordsworths' friends and patrons, when they dined at Rydal Mount.[6] For such occasions it may have been made either from

Fig 7. The Wordsworth's favourite mutton would come from the local flocks of Herd wicks. This woodcut from the Shepherds' Guide of 1810 shows how they were identified by different 'lugmarks', such as 1. fold bitted, 2. slit, 3. cropped or stoved, 4. forked, 5. shearhalved, 6. halved, 7. key bitted and 8. punched.

stock from a joint, or from meat specifically intended for producing a good broth, as in the following recipe:

To make Mutton Broth

Take the scrag end of a neck of mutton, chop it into small pieces put it into a saucepan and fill it with water. Set it over the fire, and when the scum begins to rise take it off and put in a blade or two of mace, a little French barley, or a crust of white bread to thicken it. When you have boiled your mutton that it will shake to pieces, strain your broth through a hair sieve, scum off the fat, and send it up with dry toast.[7]

> 1-1½ lb/450-675g neck of mutton, chopped in pieces
> 1½ oz/40g pearl barley   1½ tsp salt
> 2 blades mace   pepper to taste

Put the meat into a pan with 3pt/1·8l cold water, bring to the boil, remove all the scum, add the barley, mace, salt and pepper, cover and leave to simmer for about 2 hours, then skim off the fat and strain through a fine sieve into a clean pan or tureen, and serve immediately, accompanied by fresh dry toast.

[For a thicker broth, strip the meat from the bones, return it to the barley, rinse in cold water, return the meat and barley to the broth, and re-heat before serving.]

Martha Fricker provided another good recipe which used sheep shanks, these probably being the shinbones with the knuckles of the forelegs, cut from the shoulders, along with the shins cut from the back legs. The left-over bones were often recycled as pegs for holding slates on roofs, or carved into the apple-scoops used to scoop out the pulp and carry it up to the lips.

Shank broth or Jelly, cheap & nourishing

Soak twelve mutton shanks four hours then brush & scaur them very clean, put them into a saucepan with one pd of lean beef, a crust of Bread made brown [by toasting], an Onion & herbs, add four quarts of water, simmer gently five hours, then strain it off.[8]

The only soup recipe in Mary Wordsworth's book was added to it by her sister Joanna. It is very plain, despite its continental attribution.

Portuguese Vegetable Soup

Two good ... Turnips & 2 onions cut in small squares 3 pint of Water, when tender add a cupful of Rice, when that is thoroughly done ¼lb Butter a little pepper & salt. ½ hour before dinner add 3 pints of new milk & simmer until time[9]

1 onion	*1tsp salt*
1 turnip	*pinch of pepper*
3oz/75g pudding rice	*1½pt/900ml milk*
2oz/50g butter	

Cut the vegetables into small dice, stew in 1½pt/900ml water for 20 min., add the rice and simmer for a further 20 min. Add the butter, salt, pepper and milk, and simmer gently for 30 min., then serve hot.

Such broths, thickened with cheap imported rice, were popular about this period, as were very similar stews. The following example is from Coleridge's notebook of 1796, when he was still gathering useful information for his Pantisocratic life in which men would do all the cooking. It is a simple, economical and yet healthy and substantial dish, resembling the style of catering normally used in institutions such as workhouses rather than in family homes. Just like William and Dorothy's experiment of living largely on milk and potatoes two years earlier at Windy Brow, this represented a concept of plain, economical fare, rather than the food they usually ate.

[Coleridge's Stew]

Take a pound of Beef, Mutton, or Pork; cut it into small pieces; a pint of Peas; four Turnips sliced; six or seven Potatoes cut very small; four or five Onions; put to them three Quarts of Water, and let it boil about two hours and a half ... then thicken it with a pound of Rice – and boil it a quarter of an ... hour more - after which season it with salt & pepper –
N.B. better season it at first-peppering & salt the Meat &c.[10]

Artist's impression of the Wordsworth family at home. (Illustration by Peter Brears)

A cutaway view of Dove Cottage as it appeared when the Wordsworths lived there, showing the kitchen and living spaces. (Illustration by Peter Brears)

P.BREARS

Dove Cottage as it is today. The original line of upright boundary stones has been replaced with a drystone wall and the small vegetable and herb garden is situated to the left of the gate.

Rydal Mount as it appears today.

8oz/225g cubed beef, mutton or pork
8oz/225g short-grain rice   1tsp salt
8oz/225g turnips, sliced   6oz/150g peas
12oz/350g potatoes, in small cubes
8oz/225g onions, chopped   pinch ground pepper

Mix the meat, vegetables, salt and pepper in a large pan with 3pt/1·8l cold water, cover, bring to the boil, and simmer as gently as possible for 2½ hours. Stir in the rice, and continue simmering for 30 min., stirring the rice up from the bottom of the pan from time to time to prevent it sticking to the base of the pan.

The result is a very thick and plain meat, vegetable and rice stew, one that takes the bare minimum of time to prepare, occupies just one pot over a very low fire, demands little attention while cooking, and yet produces, in its original quantities, twelve pounds of economical and nourishing food from just one pound of meat.

It is probable that Herdwick mutton and Westmorland beef were slowly stewed over the fire for the Wordsworths' table, but there is no evidence to actually confirm this practice. There are a number of Joanna's recipes, however, that demonstrate the Hutchinsons' ability to produce extremely good stews, including:

Jugged Pigeons

Dress 6 pigeons, season them with beaten mace pepper & salt put them into a Jug with ½lb Butter. Stop up the Jug close, set it in a kettle of boiling water, let it boil an hour & half – put the gravy that comes from them into a pan with 1 spoonful of Wine, 1 of [mushroom?] Catchup a slice of Lemon, ½ anchovy, chopt, a bundle of sweet Herbs – boil it a little, thicken it with a little Flour, lay the Pigeons on a Dish & strain the gravy over them. [Garnish with] Mushrooms or Forcemeat[11]

6 wood pigeons, prepared   1tbs mushroom ketchup
8oz/225g butter   1tbs red or white wine
2 tsp salt   1 slice of lemon
½tsp mace   1tsp dried mixed herbs
½tsp ground black pepperflour

Mix together the salt, mace and pepper, and rub them over the breasts of the pigeons. Arrange them in a deep basin, add the butter, broken in pieces, and cover with a piece of aluminium cooking foil, pressed down over the sides all round. Set the basin on a trivet in a large pan, half-fill with boiling water, cover, return to the boil, and simmer for 1½ hours.

When cooked, pour all the liquid off into a clean glass or plastic jug, allow to settle, pour off the butter into a basin (it may be used for making any kind of savoury pastry), and the gravy into a saucepan. Add the ketchup, wine, lemon and herbs, simmer for 5 min., then add the flour beaten into the cold water. Return to the heat, stirring until it has thickened, then pass through a sieve on to the pigeons in a hot dish, and serve immediately.

Joanna also had a recipe for calf's heads, like the one Mr. Clarkson was carrying in his basket when met by William, Dorothy and Mary on New Year's Eve, 1801.[12] Unlike many Georgian versions, which serve the whole head in a dish, hers par-cooks it before stripping and cubing the meat, then converting it into a very tender and flavoursome high-quality stew. Today it may be tried using either veal or lamb:

Calf's Head

Boil the Head ½ an Hour, bone it, when cold cut it into square pieces, season it with Cayenne, white Pepper, salt & nutmeg – then cover it with Gravy, let it stew till quite enough, then put in some strong Gravy with Morrells, Mushrooms, Oysters Cockles and Mussels, (or as many of these things as you have) mix a little Butter & Flour to thicken the Soup, [i.e. the sauce] add [Mushroom?] Catchup, hard boiled Yolks of Eggs, & Force Meat Balls.[13]

By far her most interesting recipe, however, is one which must have been used at least as far back as Sockburn in the 1790s, even though written into her book around 1816. It is extremely rare to find a manuscript recipe for which there is a precise, datable description of who made it, who ate it, and what the diners thought of it, but all this information is available regarding the chicken sauce recipe from Joanna Hutchinson's book. In the summer of 1801 Coleridge used the excuse of a study-visit to Durham Cathedral library to escape from his failing marriage to the former Sarah Fricker. His real purpose, however, was to spend quality time with 'Asra', Sara Hutchinson, with whom he had fallen deeply in love. On 31st July he and Sara arrived at her brother Tom's farm at Gallow Hill, after a sixty-mile ride from Bishop Middleham. Since Coleridge's left knee was swollen and painful he was installed in the kitchen, with his leg up on a sofa, and there nursed and fed on fine meals prepared by Mary. In a letter to Sara written nine years later he could still recall how the three of them curled up on the sofa, Mary stroking his brow and Sara tickling his cheek with her eyelashes:

> The fire, Mary, you, and I at Gallow-Hill, or if, flamy, reflected in children's round faces – ah whose children? - a dog, that dog whose restless eyes oft catching the light of the fire used to watch your face, as you leaned with your head upon your hand and arm, & your feet on the fender ... Fowls at Table – the last dinner at Gallow Hill [9th August 1801], when you drest the two fowls in that delicious white Sauce ... [14]

This is the recipe that Coleridge found so delicious. It really is excellent – and eats well with either fresh-cooked vegetables or plain-boiled rice.

Chicken Sauce

The yolks of 8 Eggs hard boiled & bruised thro' a sieve, a little Lemon peel grated – a little Nutmeg Grated – or beaten mace. Mix all well with 3 or 4 spoonfuls of thick cream, then put it into melted butter made with strong white Gravy instead of Water. Squeeze some Lemon upon the Dish.[15]

1 3lb/1·4kg oven-ready chicken	2oz/50g flour
2 chicken stock cubes	2oz/50g butter
1 medium onion	3 egg yolks, separated &
4 cloves	boiled, 3 min.
¼pt/150ml double cream	1 medium carrot, peeled
juice and grated zest of a lemon	6 black peppercorns
pinch of ground nutmeg or mace	pinch of salt
bouquet garni	

Place the chicken, stock cubes, onion stuck with cloves, carrot, peppercorns, bouquet garni and salt in a pan, cover with water, cover with a lid, and simmer for 40-50 min. until tender. Remove from the heat, strain the stock into a jug, remove the vegetables, peppercorns and bouquet garni, place the chicken on a hot dish, cover with foil, and keep in a hot place until the sauce is ready.

Rub the egg yolks through a sieve. Melt the butter in a saucepan, stir in the flour, and cook gently while stirring for 1 min. Remove from the heat and gradually stir in 1pt/600ml of the stock, together with the yolks, cream, zest and nutmeg or mace. Return to the heat and stir continuously until it has boiled and thickened. Simmer for 2-3 min., add ½tsp salt and a little white pepper if required, and adjust the consistency with the remaining stock.

Remove the foil from the chicken, pour the lemon juice over it into the dish, and the sauce all over the chicken just before serving. Alternatively remove all the meat from the chicken, and arrange on a hot dish before pouring on the lemon juice and sauce, this being far more convenient to serve while still hot.

Instead of being stewed in a pan over the fire, meats could be placed in a ceramic baking dish, covered with a pastry crust, and baked in the oven, the gentler heat often producing more tender results, while still retaining all the essential juices. Dorothy's 1805 report of the twenty-month-old John Wordsworth's use of 'pie and 'taters' to signify food of every kind shows that the majority of meals served at Dove Cottage featured some form of savoury pie.[16] Most pies would probably be of their favourite mutton, but other varieties were made, such as those she made from goose giblets.

Goose-giblet pie is now a virtually forgotten dish, but up to the late nineteenth century it was relatively popular, served either alongside the roast goose, or as a separate meal in itself. Dorothy made giblet pies between late October and late November, rather than on the traditional feast of Michaelmas on September 29th, one that she baked on 11th November, 1801, apparently being eaten before the goose itself was roasted.[17] In the Lake District giblet pies included black puddings of goose or pig blood, but most better off families in the north added beef, mutton or veal steaks, which added the required bulk, and absorbed the rich flavour of the giblets, as in this version of 1812:[18]

Giblet Pie

After very nicely cleaning goose or duck giblets, stew them in a small quantity of water, onion, black pepper, and a bunch of sweet herbs, till nearly done. Let them grow cold, and if not enough to fill the dish, lay a beef, veal, or two or three mutton steaks at the bottom. Put the liquor of the stew to bake with the above, and when the pie is baked, pour into it a large tea-cupful of cream. Sliced potatoes added to it, eat extremely well.[19]

Goose giblets	4oz/100g flour
1 small onion, chopped	2oz/50g lard
pinch ground black pepper	pinch of salt
1 bouquet garni	¼pt/150ml cream
12-16oz/350-450g beef or mutton steaks, trimmed	
1 large peeled potato (optional)	

Prepare the giblets by removing the gall-bladder from the liver, squeezing and washing the heart, skinning and removing the pipe from the neck, opening and washing the gizzard, and tearing away its thick lining. Put the giblets into a small pan with the onion, pepper, salt and bouquet garni, barely cover with water, and simmer very gently for 30 min. before removing from the heat and leaving to cool.

Rub the lard into the flour and a pinch of salt, and mix in about 2tbs cold water to form the pastry. Place the steaks in the bottom of a 1½ pt/900ml baking dish, remove the neck bone and chop the giblets into pieces, laying these on top, and almost cover with the strained giblet stock. If required, the potato may now be sliced and laid on top.

Roll out the pastry, use it to cover the baking dish, having moistened the rim, cut a hole in the centre, and use the trimmings to make a raised border, pressed down with a fork. Bake at 200°C, 400°F, Gas mark 2 for a further hour, before serving hot.

Dorothy left no recipe for the veal pies she made in July 1802, but below is the Fricker version:[20]

Veal Patties

Make a short crust, and roll it out thick, take the kidney part of a very fat loin of veal – Chop the kidney, veal and fat very small all together – season it with mace, pepper and salt to your taste – fill your Patties and cover them with a Crust – colour them with the yolk of an egg & bake them.[21]

To make 6 patties take:

1lb/450g veal or lamb, including a kidney
1tsp salt   *½tsp mace*
¼tsp pepper   *1 egg, beaten*
Shortcrust pastry made from:
8oz/225g flour,   *4oz/100g lard,*
a pinch of salt, and about 4 tbs cold water.

Finely chop/coarsely mince the meat, and mix in the salt, pepper and mace. Use ⅔ of the pastry to line six 3ins/7·5cm straight-sided small pie or deep bun tins, fill almost to the brim with the meat, brush the edges with the beaten egg, and pinch on the lids, each having a hole cut through its centre. Brush the top with egg, place on a baking sheet and bake at 200° C, 400°F, Gas mark 6 for 10 min., then reduce to 150°C, 300°F, Gas mark 2 for a further 25-30 min. Allow to cool a little, and the juices to be absorbed into the meat, before removing from their tins. Either serve immediately, or when cold, accompanied by pickles.

Joanna appears to have made really good hare pies, which again work well with venison:

Hare Pie

Cut a hare in pieces, season it well, put it in a Jug with ½lb of Butter, cover it close, set it in a pan of boiling water, let it stew an hour & half – make force meat of bread crumbs, bacon scraped & a little of the liver & sweet Herbs &c. season it high – put the Hare into the dish with the gravy that comes out of it, & the force meat – when cov [ere]d an hour will bake it.[22]

1 hare, drawn & skinned	*grated zest of ½ lemon*
1½tsp each marjoram & thyme	*8oz/225g butter*
2 rashers streaky bacon	*2 anchovy fillets*
½tsp ground black pepper	*¼tsp salt*
⅓ of a nutmeg grated	*1 egg, beaten*
6oz/150g fresh white breadcrumbs	*2tbs red wine*
Shortcrust pastry made from	
12oz/320g flour,	*6oz/150g lard,*
a pinch of salt and about 5 tbs cold water.	

Remove all the meat from the carcase, carefully taking out all the sinews etc. and cut into cubes about an inch across. Put them into a ceramic basin, along with the butter cut into small pieces, and cover with a piece of cooking foil pressed down tightly over the rim and outside. Place the basin on a trivet in a large pan, pour in boiling water until half-way up the basin, cover, return to the boil, and simmer for 1½ hours, stirring the contents after 30 min. to separate the pieces of hare.

Meanwhile make the pastry and set aside to rest in a cool place. Finely chop the bacon and anchovies, and mix into the breadcrumbs along with the remaining dry ingredients, then work in the egg and wine to produce a smooth forcemeat. Roll this into balls about ¾ins/2cm diameter.

Pour the hare stock from the basin into a glass or plastic jug, leave to settle for a few minutes, then pour off the clear butter into a separate vessel. Arrange the drained hare in a large pie-dish, along with the forcemeat balls, and almost fill with the stock and a little of the butter. Roll out the pastry and use to cover the pie-dish, having moistened its rim. Use the trimmings to add a raised edge, a border to a hole cut in the centre, and any leaves etc. as decoration. Brush with milk and bake at 220°C, 425°F, Gas mark 7 for 20 min., then reducing the temperature to 180°C, 350°F, Gas mark 4 for a further 20 min., then serve immediately.

As well as these rich meat pies, Joanna made others of bacon and egg, the predecessors of the thin, double-crusted plate pies of the later nineteenth and twentieth centuries.

Egg & Bacon Pie

Steep a few thin slices of Bacon in water, beat 8 Eggs with some milk put the Bacon on the Bottom of the Dish Pour the eggs over it season it with pepper & salt cover & bake it, in a moderate oven.[23]

4oz/100g flour	*6 eggs, beaten*
2oz/50g lard	*½tsp salt*
4 rashers bacon, soaked in water for 15 min.	

Rub the lard into the flour, with a pinch of salt, and mix in about 2 tbs cold water, to make the pastry. Roll out to fit a 1½pt/900ml baking dish, cut a small round hole in the centre, surrounding it with a ring of pastry, moistened, and stuck in position.

Line the dish with the drained bacon, beat the salt into the eggs, and pour on top. Use a little of the egg to wet the rim of the dish, place the pastry lid on top, trim the edges, and use the trimmings to make a raised border, forking the top to press it into position. Bake in an oven pre-heated to 200°C, 400°F, Gas mark 6 for 20 min., then reduce to 150°C, 300°F, Gas mark 2 for a further 30 min., then serve hot.

Joints of meat such as mutton, sirloin of beef, goose or turkey were roasted before the radiant heat of the kitchen fire, rotating there and being basted until done to a turn.[24] There is neither documentary nor physical evidence for any particular kind of spit mechanism. The most probable method would have been to suspend the joint on a twisted skein of twine, and spin it by hand at frequent intervals, to maintain its motion. The resulting roast was well worth the effort of watching and turning, since it gave far more delicately-flavoured and moist results than are achieved today. The Hutchinsons must have been in the habit of having a roast suckling pig for dinner on special occasions, this being amongst the finest of all spit-roasts.

The Wordsworths' friend Charles Lamb wrote one of the most enthusiastic, enjoyable and saliva-producing passages in the whole of English culinary literature in its praise. His *'Dissertation upon Roast Pig'* celebrates the incomparable flavour;

> 'of the crisp, tawny, well-watched, not over-roasted crackling, as it is well called the very teeth are invited to

their share of the pleasure at this banquet in overcoming the coy, brittle resistance with the adhesive oleaginous O call it not fat!, but an indefinable sweetness growing up to it the tender blossoming of fat & the lean, no lean, but a kind of animal mannu or rather fat and lean so blended and running into each other that both make but one ambrosial result, or common substance'

This would have been a far too luxurious dish for the Wordsworths' table but, when the Hutchinsons cooked it, Joanna made the following as soon as it came off the spit:

Pig Sauce

Chop the brains a little with the gravy from the Pig & a little bit of anchovy a little salt, a spoonful of white wine a slice of Lemon, put all into melted butter [white sauce] & heat it over the Fire. [25]

Broiling also used the radiant heat of the fire, but employed the narrow horizontal bars of the gridiron to hold steaks and other relatively thin pieces of meat a few inches above the glowing coals. Dorothy used this method to cook beefsteaks, mutton chops etc., and may have broiled rashers of ham and bacon in the same way.[26] This would certainly have produced ideally crisp results, but would have wasted all the lard or bacon-dripping. For this reason ham and bacon was usually fried to produce sufficient fat for frying the eggs etc. In 1800 Dorothy was buying her bacon, but from around 1812 the family was breeding pigs to home-cure as bacon and ham.[27] Mary's recipe book provides the following instructions: The word 'genel' is not in general use now, but meant an entry, or a passage, especially between houses.

Pickle for Hams

To each ham 1lb of bay salt, ½lb of common salt 2oz salt Peta, 1oz of black pepper beat all these very fine & rub upon the ham let it lay 4 days then pour over it 1½lb of Treacle & let it stay a month turning it every day then put the ham into cold water for 12 hours when it has hung 2 months cover it well up in a brown paper bag & keep it in a genel or dry cellar: if it moulds it will be good.
Mrs Hugessen[28]

The Frickers' meanwhile used a simpler basic method, but then brushed the ham with a crude vinegar made from wood, called pyroligneous acid, to replicate the effect of smoking in a smoke-loft. A good example of such a loft can still be seen above the kitchen fireplace at Town End, Troutbeck.

Smoking Hams &c

Salt your meat in the usual way taking care to put the salt well in, & to turn the meat in the brine once every day. At the end of three or four weeks hang the meat up to drain 24 hours, then with a brush, such as is used for oiling Harness's dipped in the concentrated rough Pyroligneous Acid, smear the meat well over, and hang it up in an airy place. One application of the Acid is generally sufficient, but a second or third will produce a more powerful Westphalia [ham] flavour.[29]

Many local households used salting and sometimes subsequent smoking to preserve legs of mutton or joints of beef, especially for boiling over the winter months. There is no evidence that the Wordsworths did this, since they bought in, rather than bred, their butcher-meat. It would almost certainly have been practised by the stock-breeding Hutchinsons such as their great-uncle Thomas, who could produce sheep weighing seventeen and a half stone, or brother John, who exhibited his fat heifer at the Smithfield Christmas show of 1822.[30] Coleridge was interested in the practice, recording the following method in 1799.

[Salt Beef]

Thin flank of Beef is taken out, sprinkled with salt petre n. b. not with common Salt. to lay a fortnight, turning it every day it must be & tied very close boil it three or 4 hours according to the size till quite tender then press it with a small weight[31]

For keeping over winter, the salted but uncooked joints were hung up in a secure, well-ventilated location. When staying at an inn at Ingleby in 1800 Coleridge particularly noted a large buttock of beef hanging up in the thatch of the living room, from which portions could be cut, soaked and boiled as required.[32]

Moving on from meat to fish, there is very little evidence for the

Fig 8. In Westmorland these long-horned cattle were still the main source of beef for the local market

ways in which it was cooked at Dove Cottage. Presumably those caught by William, his brother John etc. were simply cleaned and either fried or grilled, still one of the best of all methods. In August 1800, however, Dorothy recorded that she had stuffed two small pike, and baked a loaf.[33] Since the oven would be hot, this suggests that she baked them, a much more reliable method than either simmering or roasting. Most of the baked pike recipes of this period recommended very rich stuffings with flavours which permeated the delicate flesh as it slowly cooked:

To Stuff and Bake & Pike

Having scaled and cleaned the fish without cutting open much of the breast, stuff them with a maigre forcemeat made thus; Beat yolks of eggs, a few oysters bearded and chopped, and two boned anchovies & grated bread, minced parsley, and a bit of eschalot or an onion, mace pounded, black pepper, all-spice, and salt. Mix these in proper proportions; and having beat a good piece of butter in a stew-pan, stir them in it over the fire till the consistence of a thick batter, then adding more & flour if necessary. Fill the fish, and sew up the slit. Bake them in a moderate oven, basting with plenty of butter, and sticking butter all over them, serve pike with anchovy sauce [made from the juices from the baking dish, thickened with a roux][34]

> *1 pike, scaled, cleaned, opened at the breast, rinsed in cold water, and dried with a cloth or paper towel*
>
> | | |
> |---|---|
> | *4 egg yolks, beaten* | *¼tsp mace* |
> | *8oz/225g fresh white breadcrumbs* | *¼tsp allspice* |
> | *1 medium onion, finely chopped* | *½tsp salt* |
> | *¼tsp ground black pepper* | *4oz/100g butter* |
> | *4 oysters, bearded & chopped* | *4 anchovy fillets* |
> | *2tsp chopped parsley* | |

Melt the butter in a saucepan, stir in all the ingredients, except the pike, and stir over a gentle heat until thickened. Adjust the thickness with either a little more butter, or flour, as necessary to produce a thick but moist stuffing.

Pack this into the pike, sew up the opening, place in a large baking dish, and cook at 180°C, 350°F, Gas mark 4 for 30-40 min., regularly basting with butter.

Joanna Hutchinson's only fish recipe is for eels, traditionally caught in the north country by using a special multi-pronged spear called a glave. Like pike, they are quite a challenge to prepare for the table, the skins being both slippery and tough. She merely directs the cook to 'Case the Eels', that is to skin them, but this is easier said than done. The best instructions for this process are given in Bill Fowler of Eskdale's *Countryman's Cooking* of 1965:

> If you have a big eel that you want to cook yourself, you go about it like this: Get a piece of strong string, about two feet long, and tie the ends together. Pass the knot through the loop at the other end, so as to form a noose. Put this noose around the eel's neck, just below the head, pull tight, and hang the eel up by a strong nail. With a sharp knife, cut round the skin just below the string; now take hold of the edge of this skin with a pair of pliers. A strong, long tug downwards will remove the skin entirely inside out. Cut off the head [and] clean out the guts.

Joanna then goes on to remove the bones, to produce long fillets which are then collared in a similar method to that used for soused herrings:

Eels to collar

Case the Eels, cut off the Heads, slit open the bellies, cut off the Fins, & take out the Guts & bones lay them flat on the Back, grate over them a Nutmeg, two or 3 blades of mace beaten fine a little Pepper & salt strew them over a little Sage & parsley shred fine roll them up tight in a cloth & bind it well.

If a middle sized eel boil it ¾ of an Hour in salt & water Hang it up all Night to drain add to the Pickle a pint of vinegar, & a few Pepper Corns, a sprig of sweet Marjoram boil it 10 minutes next day take off the Cloth & put the Eels into it.[35]

It would be surprising to find no mention of char in the Wordsworth papers, for this trout-like fish, found in Windermere, Coniston Water, and a number of other local lakes and tarns, had been caught and preserved locally for centuries. Originally they were baked in butter in large pies. The Fleming account books of 1665 describe how they were 'sent up to London only between Xmas and Easter by reason ye Fish is at ye best and ye weather ye coolest for carryage'. And in March 1663; 'Ye carryage of 2 Pies to London (to ye Lord Arlington and Joseph Williamson Esq) Weight 7 stone 6lbs ye sum of £1.'[36] By 1675 tinplate pie crusts were also in use, but the early eighteenth century saw the introduction of char-pots, many being made at the Liverpool delftware potteries. Broad and circular, they had short vertical walls around which a number of colourful char were painted. At the opening of the nineteenth century around 1,800 such pots were required every year to pot around 10,800 char, illustrating the importance of this seasonal local industry.

In 1804 the Wordsworths had enjoyed broiled char fresh out of the tarn at Seathwaite in the Duddon Valley, but in later years they appear to have purchased some potted char, arranging them to be dispatched to Thomas Monkhouse in London.[37] In March 1813 Sara informed him that he was being sent 'in the Box a Pot of Chars which I hope will be acceptable to you & The Pots were not as large as I supposed, therefore I send two I should be glad to hear of their safe arrival.'[38] Sara also potted the fish caught by her family's menfolk. One Saturday her brother Henry 'went off again this morning before [I] was up so eager is he after his fishing He brought a fine lot which I potted, or rather

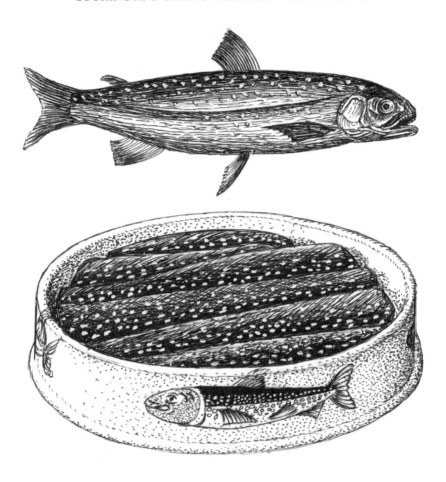

Fig 9. The char caught in lakes such as Windermere and Coniston Water (top) were cleaned, salted, baked, and packed into char pots (bottom) ready for despatch all over England. In the early nineteenth century the local trade required about 1,800 of these pots every year.

intended to pot but Mary Anne, being in love, chose after they were baked to leave them in the way of the dog, who dispatched the greater part.'[39]

Recipes for potting char were given by a number of contemporary authors, such as Mrs Raffald of Manchester, Mrs Burton, wife of the Rector of Windermere, and others. They all use very similar methods, only varying in the variety and quantity of their spicing, the following giving excellent results.[40]

To Pot Char, or Trout

1½lb/625g char or trout, after having had their heads, tails,
fins and backbones removed.

1-2oz/25-50g salt	*1tsp ground mace*
1½tsp ground white pepper	*½ a nutmeg, grated*
¼tsp ground cloves	*8oz/225g butter*

Sprinkle the salt and pepper inside and outside the fish, place in a dish, and leave overnight in a cool place. Put the butter in a saucepan with ¼ pt/150ml water, bring to the boil, and when all the butter is melted, also leave in a cool place overnight.

Next morning, pour the butter into a sieve, discard the brine, and heat the butter in a saucepan to evaporate the remaining water. Remove from the heat when the bubbles have subsided, and then set aside.

Rapidly rinse each fish to remove the brine, wipe dry with a cloth, and sprinkle with the mixed spices inside and out. Keeping the skin sides outwards, pack each double fillet into a baking dish, cover first with the clarified butter, then with a piece of cooking foil, and bake at 110°C, 225°F, Gas mark ¼ for four hours. Remove from the oven, and pour all the butter off into a glass jug. Pack the fish into a clean baking or serving dish about 1½ ins/4cm deep, arranging them head-end to tail-end, backs upward, as closely as possible. Pour in the melted clarified butter from the jug, carefully excluding the dull liquid beneath, and leave in a cool place to set, gently pressing down the fillets with the back of a fork to keep as much as possible under the butter.

Keep in a cool place for 2-3 days if then required for use, or cover with a ¼ins/1cm layer of more clarified butter if intended to be kept for a longer period, always storing in the cool.

The butter-sealed char pots were then wrapped in paper and packed into casks ready for transport to London and elsewhere. The wooded hills of Furness had a long-established cask and hoop-making industry with which William was intimately familiar, since John Tyson, husband of his Hawkshead 'dame', was a manufacturer of char-pot casks.[41]

Perhaps the most unusual recipe for cooking fish is the following example from Joanna Hutchinson. It simmers trout in seasoned beer and then thickens the liquid with egg yolks and the grated brown crust of a loaf to form a sauce. The bitterness of the hops, browned crusts and an onion completely overwhelms rather than complements the delicate flavour of the fish, and is little improved by the sharp acidity of the vinegar or lemon juice added at the end. Joanna must have enjoyed it, otherwise she would not have taken the trouble to enter Mrs. Montague's recipe into her book, but even around 1816 it must have been something of an acquired taste.

Receipt to stew Fish

Take half a pint of Ale or Porter, mix with it an onion chopped small and as much Parsley as will cover a Table spoon chopped very fine, a little salt, Cayenne Pepper, common Pepper, Anchovy Liquor or Catchup, or a little good gravy; Take your Fish and clean and wash them very well, cutting off the Fins and Heads; roll them in Flour and put them in a stew pan with some Butter the size of a Walnut broke into two or three pieces and laid in the bottom of the pan, rasp the upper crust of a loaf and dust the fish over with the brown raspings, then cover the fish with the ingredients above mentioned, and let the whole stew twenty minutes very gently; before the fish is dished, beat up the yolks of three Eggs, and mix them with the gravy, but do not set the fish again upon the fire after the Eggs are added:

Take the fish carefully out, pour the gravy (which ought to be thick) over it, and rasp the whole over with brown raspings, little vinegar or Lemon juice is an improvement, – the ingredients are for three good sized Trouts, they must be increased in proportion.

Mrs Montague[42]

3 trout, cleaned, head, tail & fins removed
2tsp mushroom ketchup or anchovy sauce
1tbs chopped parsley
2-3oz/50-75g grated bread crust
pinch cayenne pepper
1-2tbs vinegar or lemon juice
1 small onion, finely chopped
½oz/12g butter
flour for dusting
½pt/300ml brown ale
¼tsp salt
3 egg yolks, beaten
pinch black pepper

Just melt the butter in the bottom of a wide pan or a small frying pan, dust the trout with flour, and lay on top. Sprinkle with the parsley, salt, peppers and onion, pour in the ketchup or sauce with the ale, and cover with half the breadcrumbs. Cover, and simmer very gently for 10-12 minutes. Remove the pan from the heat, beat some of the cooking liquid into the egg yolks, return this to the fish, and stir in to thicken. Using a slice, transfer the trout to a hot dish, pour the sauce on top, cover with the remaining crumbs, sprinkle with the vinegar or lemon juice, and serve immediately.

There are no details describing how the Wordsworths cooked their vegetables, but it would be safe to assume that they prepared and plain-boiled them in salted water in the usual manner. The only recipe that has survived is the following version of creamed mushrooms, which Joanna served with 'sippets', fingers of fried or toasted bread set around the dish, but for today's use they are best piled onto hot buttered toast.

Stewed Mushrooms

Peel the Mushrooms & put them into a pan with a little water let them stew ¼ an hour, then put in a little pepper & salt, flour & Butter to make the gravy thick as Cream, before it is dished up put in a large spoonful of cream & stir it over the fire. Sippets.[43]

1lb/450g mushrooms	*½oz/12g butter*
½tsp salt	*½oz/12g flour*
pinch of pepper	*1tbs double cream*

Pull the stalks from the mushrooms, and wipe clean. Peel the caps by pulling the skin off upwards from its inner rim. Put all the mushrooms into a pan with ¾pt/450ml cold water, bring to the boil, and simmer for 15 min. before stirring in the salt, pepper and flour rubbed into a soft paste with the butter. Stir gently for a further 5 min. until the sauce has thickened, adding the cream just before serving. The edge of the dish may be decorated with sippets in the form of small triangles cut out of fried bread or toast.

Chapter Four

OF COLD PUDDINGS

Cold puddings were amongst the most luxurious dishes in Georgian cookery, partly because of the nature of their ingredients, such as rich cream, sugar and fruits, and partly due to the level of skill and length of time required to bring some of them to successful completion. It is interesting to note that some two-thirds of such recipes in the Wordsworth Trust's collections are from the Frickers. They represent the type of cookery which they would be expected to prepare in their Bristol home, and probably continued to make when running their own establishments. The recipes of Mary Wordsworth, and Joanna Hutchinson, though fewer in number and being a little plainer, still demonstrate that they too could produce excellent cold puddings whenever required.

When all these recipes were carefully noted down, the food manufacturing industry was still in its infancy, all wives and housekeepers still expecting to have to start every dish from its basic ingredients. Since there were no pre-prepared gelatins on the market, making something as simple as a clear well-flavoured jelly usually started off by buying in a 'gang' of four calf's feet from the butcher. After being cleaned, boiled for hours, chilled, and separated from both sediment and scum, their gelatinous stock was flavoured, clarified with the whites and shells of eggs, and finally filtered through a conical flannel filter-bag. The whole process might take several days. In the modernised version below gelatin has been substituted for the calf's feet, but the jellies retain their original flavours. To obtain good results it is essential to know how to mould jellies. It is easiest to use moulds made of tin-lined copper or aluminium. When the jelly has been set by standing overnight in a cool place, quickly dip the mould into warm water, which will release its contents. Working rapidly, hold the jelly mould at 45° in one hand, wet the other hand, the flat surface of the jelly and the serving dish, and slowly rotate and invert the mould until the full weight of the jelly is resting on the front of the fingers of the free hand. Hold the mould just above the serving dish, and pull the fingers away, allowing the jelly to slip down onto it. As the dish is already wet, the jelly may be slid into position, where it will soon stick, as the wetness is absorbed. When using moulds made of plastic, pottery or glass, dipping the mould in warm water rarely releases all the jelly before substantial parts of it have melted. The solution is to smear the inside of the mould with an extremely thin coating of butter, and pour in the jelly solution when cold, but not at the point of setting. This stops the jelly adhering to the mould, so there is no need to dunk the mould in warm water before proceeding as just described above.

Calf Feet Jelly

Wash & clean the Feet to a gang [ie 4 of them] *put 4qts of water, boil it down half, when cold take off the Fat. To a qt. of stock put a pint of white wine, a little brandy, the whites & shells of 4 Eggs beaten, some Cinnamon, the juice & Rinds of 2 Lemons. Sweeten it with loaf Sugar, boil all together 'till it breaks then run it thro' a bag (return it 'till it is clear) into Glasses* [1]

Calf's Feet Jelly

Boil 4 feet greatly in 5 quarts of water & strain it & when cold take off the fat, & scum the jelly from the sediment, put it into a saucepan with 1 quart of Madeira. 1 gill of Brandy, the rind & juice of 2 lemons, the whites of 6 eggs beaten to a froth & their shells broken small, boil it ten minutes, put in a small piece of cinnamon & sweeten it to your taste. Dip a Flannel jelly-bag into hot water, & keep stirring the jelly gently through it until it runs quite clear. [2]

7tsp/gelatin or 7 leaves	*¼pt/150ml Madeira*
1ins/2·5cmstick cinnamon	*3tbs brandy*
pared zest and juice ½ lemon	*3tbs sugar*

Mix the lemon juice with ¼pt/150ml water and strain into a pan. Add the Madeira, sprinkle and then stir in the gelatin (or broken up leaves). Soak for 5 min. then add the remaining ingredients and heat gently while stirring until it steams, and all is dissolved. Remove the pan from the stove, cover, and wrap in towels to infuse for 1 hour. Pour through a sieve into a measuring jug, make up to 1pt/600ml with cold water, stir thoroughly, and pour into a prepared mould, leaving this in a cool place overnight to set.

The only other gelling agent was isinglass, the swimming bladder or 'sound' of certain fish, particularly the sturgeon. Once cleaned and dried, it was formed into various shapes called 'book', 'pipe' or 'ribbon' for sale through high quality grocer's shops. Though much more expensive than calf's feet, it could simply be soaked, simmered and strained to produce a firm clear jelly, ready for sweetening and flavouring. The recipe below demonstrates how Georgian cooks were able to extract and retain as much as possible of the flavour of their expensive ingredients, all to make something we would now find virtually indistinguishable from a modern packet jelly.

Orange Jelly

Grate the rind of two Seville and two China oranges and two lemons, squeeze the juice of three of each and strain then add a quarter of a pound of lump sugar and a quarter of a pint of water boiled till near candying. Have ready a quart of isinglass jelly made with two ounces, put the syrup to it, and boil it once up but do not stir it after it begins to warm – Strain it through a flannel jelly bag dipped in hot water and let it spend half an hour to settle, before it is put into the Mould.[3]

7tsp gelatin	*1½ lemons*
1 large Seville & 1 large sweet orange	*2oz/50g sugar*

Sprinkle, then stir the gelatin into ½pt/300ml cold water, leave to soak for 5 min. warm over the stove or microwave for1 min. until it has dissolved, then make up to ¾pt/450ml with cold water, and set aside.

Grate the zest off the oranges and a lemon, place in a pan with the sugar and 3.5fl.oz/100ml water, then boil rapidly for 15 min. and pour into the gelatin mixture. Line a sieve with a freshly rinsed and wrung-out piece of cloth, pour in the mixture, and let it filter through once or twice until it is virtually clear, and set aside until cold, but not set. Then pour into a 1pt/600ml mould and leave in a cool place overnight to set.

Blancmange, literally 'white-food', originated as a sweet chicken paté in medieval kitchens, then slowly transformed itself through the centuries to emerge as the cornflour 'shape' or mould of former school dinners and communal teas. It achieved its most delicious form during the eighteenth and early nineteenth centuries when it was a cool and delicate almond milk and cream jelly, ideal for all summertime entertainments. Since the bitter almonds in the original recipes contained potentially dangerous levels of Prussic acid, they have been substituted by almond essence in the up-dated version below. It eats particularly well when accompanied by the Wordsworths' preserved damsons. (See page 141)

Blanc Mange with Isinglass

Put 1oz of picked Isinglass to a pint of water with a bit of Cinnamon & boil till the Isinglass is melted, put to it ¾ of a pint of Cream, two ounces of sweet almonds and six bitter almonds, blanched and beaten, and a bit of lemon peel, sweeten it – stir it over the fire, and let it boil, then strain it, & stir it till it is cool – squeeze in the juice of ½ a lemon & put it in moulds – always wet moulds before you put in the blancmange. [4]

Blanc Mange

Pour a pint of boiling water over 2oz of Isinglass, when dissolved strain it off put to it ¼lb sweet almonds and 12 bitter beaten and beaten fine in a mortar with 3 spoonful of orange flower water & a pint of cream – put in sugar to the taste, boil ¼ hour stirring all the time – strain it off, stirring till it becomes thick – put it into moulds. [5]

5tsp gelatin	½tsp almond essence
2oz/50g flaked almonds	3tbs sugar
4½tsp orange flower water	½pt/300ml cream

Sprinkle, then stir, the gelatin into ½pt /300ml cold water, leave to soak for 5 min., then heat on the stove, or microwave for 1 min., and stir until it has completely dissolved. Blend this liquid with the almonds until they form a smooth cream, then add the remaining ingredients. Stir over a gentle heat until it rises in the pan, then set aside to cool. Rub the inside of a jelly or blancmange mould with a little butter, making sure to cover every part, pour in the blancmange when cold but not set, then leave in a cold

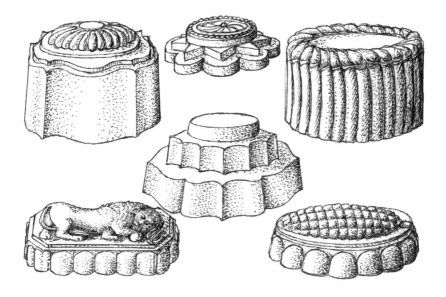

Fig 10. Blancmanges were very popular in the late Georgian period. These are some of the shapes produced by Wedgwood's moulds.

place for a few hours or overnight before serving.

In contrast to blancmange, jaunemange was 'yellow-food', its colour coming from the addition of egg yolks. Its alternative and perhaps less fashionable name was yellow flummery. Essentially a set custard, its initially bland and creamy flavours subside to leave a more mature lemon and wine after-taste, making it a good accompaniment to either stewed or preserved fruit.

Yellow Flummery

2oz of Isinglass beat & open it, put it into a bowl & pour a pint of boiling water upon it. Cover it up till almost cold, then add a pint of White Wine the juice of 2 & the rind of one Lemon, Yolks of 8 Eggs well beaten – sweeten to the taste, put it into a tossing Pan, stir it & when it boils strain it thro' a fine sieve– when almost cold put it into moulds.[6]

Jaune Mange

*Two of Isinglass – pint of boiling water, when dissolved add ½
pint of wine – yolks of 8 eggs & the rinds of two [? Lemons]
sweeten and let it boil, then pour into moulds* [7]

4tsp gelatin　　　　　　　　　*yolks of 4 eggs, beaten*
¼pt/150ml white wine　　　　　*pared zest of a lemon*
3-5tbs sugar, according to the sweetness/sharpness of the wine.

Put the wine, lemon zest, yolks and sugar into a pan with
½pt/300ml water, sprinkle on and then stir in the gelatin,
and leave for 5 min. Stir all together over a gentle heat until
hot and beginning to thicken, but do not allow to boil, then
strain through a sieve into a jug, and set aside until cold
but not set. Turn into prepared moulds and leave in a cool
place overnight to set.

To avoid the troublesome use of gelatin, some later Georgian cooks
began to replace it with a variety of starchy ingredients. This was the
start of the slow transformation of the blancmange from a smooth,
luscious delicacy into the solid, heavy-textured cornflour 'shape' of
modern times. Martha Fricker's recipe clearly illustrates this change:

Receipt for imitation Blancmange

*Take a quart of a pd of ground Rice a quarter of an ounce of Bitter
Almonds beaten fine, mix them smooth in rather less than a pint of
good milk, put pounded white sugar to your taste. When put into
moulds it will turn out stiff* [8]

4oz/100g ground rice　　　　　*3tbs sugar*
1pt/600ml full cream milk
1tsp almond flavouring, to replace the dangerous use of
　　　　　　　　　　　　　　　　　　　　bitter almonds

Mix the ingredients in a pan, stir over a medium heat
until boiling, simmer for 5 min., stirring continuously to
prevent it from burning, then drop it into a freshly-rinsed
mould, excluding any air-pockets, and level the top.
Leave to cool for a few hours, then turn out on to a dish,

and serve with either preserved (tinned) or fresh stewed fruit, or with fruit jams.

Smooth, rich and satisfying, cream provided an ideal basis for any number of cold puddings, in which its essential qualities were enhanced by the addition of contrasting bitter-sweet or sharp flavours. The blend of lemon, orange flower water and caramelised sugar make this a particularly good crème brûleé:

Burnt Cream

Take a Pint of Cream, boil it with sugar & a little lemon peel shred fine – then beat the yolks of six, and the whites of 4 eggs separately – when the cream is cooled, put in the eggs, with a spoonful of orange flower water & one of fine flour – mix it over the fire, keep stirring it till it is thick, then put it into a dish. When cold, sift ¼ of a pound of sugar all over; hold a hot Salamander over it, and when it is very brown, and looks as if a glass Plate were put over your Cream.[9]

1pt/600ml double cream	*1tbs flour*
4 yolks and 2 whites of egg	*2tbs sugar*
1tbs orange flower water	*½tsp grated lemon zest*
For the glaze: 4oz/100g caster sugar	

Simmer the cream, 2tbs sugar and zest very gently for 5 min. and leave to cool. Beat together the yolks, and whites, the orange flower water and the flour, stir into the cream, and stir over a gentle heat until it has just thickened, then pour into a heatproof dish, and set aside until perfectly cold. 2-3 hours before serving spread the sugar evenly across the surface and place under a hot pre-heated grill for 2-3 minutes until it has melted and taken on a colour, then remove, cool and chill.

Instead of setting the cream with eggs, it could also be transformed into a very smooth, thick curd by acidifying it with lemon juice and leaving it in a cool place overnight. Joanna's basic recipe is quite straightforward, but optimistic in its claim to achieve a sufficiently firm set to allow it to be turned out like a blancmange. In practice it is probably best to substitute the mould with a serving dish.

Lemon Solid

Grate the rind of a Lemon into a Dish and squeeze the juice upon it, boil a pint of thick [double] cream and sweeten it [2-3tbs sugar]. set the mould on the ground and strain the cream into it boiling hot, stir it well, let it stand all night, in the morning turn it out and stick it with Candied Orange &c.[10]

This could be converted into a Swiss or Stone Cream merely by adding cooked or preserved fruits in the dish with the lemon juice as in the following versions from Martha Fricker's recipe books:

Swiss Cream

Lay apricots or plums in the bottom of a dish, squeeze the juice of a lemon and the rind grated upon them, boil a pint of thick cream, and sweeten it to your taste; Set your dish in a cool place, and strain the cream very hot into it, let it remain all night, & ornament it with candied orange.[11]

Stone Cream

Put into the Dish you intend to send to Table Apricots, or other sweetmeats, cut small, & Three spoonfuls of lemon or orange juice, with a little of the peel grated –
Then take a pint of Cream, ¼ of an ounce of Isinglass, a little cinnamon and a few lumps of sugar, boil it till the Isinglass is quite dissolved – Then strain it into a jug that has a spout and when about the heat of new milk pour over the sweetmeats, round the Dish – it should be made some hours before it is wanted.[12]

1 standard tin of apricots, drained & chopped
3tbs strained fresh orange or lemon juice
grated zest of either an orange or a lemon
1pt/600ml single cream   4tbs sugar
2ins/5cm stick cinnamon   5tsp gelatin

Arrange the apricots as an even layer across the base of a large dish, and sprinkle on the orange or lemon juice and zest. Put the cream, cinnamon and sugar into a pan, sprinkle and then stir in the gelatin, and leave for 5 min.

Heat gently while stirring until all is melted, but not to boiling point, then remove from the heat, leave until tepid, pour into a jug, and pour onto the apricots all over, from the height of a foot or two/30-60cm, to ensure it blends with the lemon juice. Leave in a cold place, preferably overnight, before serving.

Other creams were eaten in a semi-liquid state, and so were served either in dishes and bowls, or in individual custard glasses. For present day use they are most conveniently served in wine glasses and accompanied by sponge finger biscuits for dunking.

Custards

Take 1 Pint of Cream and 1 of new milk – set them over the fire with a little sugar, Cinnamon, Lemon Peel, 4 ounces of sweet almonds and 1 of bitter blanched and chopped small, when it has boiled, take it off the fire and add the yolks and whites of 4 eggs well beaten, then set it over the fire again till thick enough and take care to keep stirring it all one way & not to let it boil – pour it into a jug and when cold take out the Cinnamon and Lemon Peel and put a tablespoonful of Brandy & 2 of Madeira. [13]

½pt/300ml double cream	*½pt/300ml milk*
2oz/50g almonds, finely chopped	*½tsp almond essence*
2-3tbs sugar	*2 eggs beaten*
1 stick cinnamon	*½tbs brandy*
pared zest of ½ lemon	*1tbs Madeira*

Mix all the ingredients (except the eggs, brandy & Madeira) in a pan, simmer for 5 min., stirring to prevent it from burning. Remove from the heat, and pour a little onto the eggs, stirring vigorously to prevent curdling. Stir the egg mixture into the contents of the pan, return to a very gentle heat and stir continuously until just thickened, but not curdled. Remove from the heat and pour into a jug. Take out the lemon zest and cinnamon stick, stir in the brandy and Madeira, and pour into wine glasses to cool.

Lemon Cream

Take a pint of thick cream and put to it the yolks of two eggs well beaten, four ounces of fine sugar, and the thin rind of a lemon, boil it up, then stir it till almost cold, put the juice of a lemon in a dish or bowl, and pour the Cream upon it, stirring it until quite cold.[14]

> *1pt/600ml double cream*   *2oz/50g sugar*
> *pared zest and juice of 1 lemon*   *yolks of 2 eggs, beaten*

Mix the cream, yolks, zest and sugar in a pan and stir while heating almost to boiling point, then set aside to cool, stirring frequently to prevent the formation of a tough skin on top. When almost cold, pour onto the lemon juice either in a dish or bowl. Alternatively stir in the lemon juice and pour into individual wine glasses, and leave to go perfectly cold before serving.

The following cold pudding is one of only four in the recipe book kept by Mary Wordsworth. Essentially a moulded rice pudding, it is quite different from anything we would recognise by that name today. It is flavoured with salt rather than sugar to provide a relatively bland foil for the sharper, richer flavours of marmalade, jam or stewed fruits. In this it takes on a similar role to that of the bread in a jam sandwich.

Rice [Mould]

Wash and put a little clear water to it, set it in the oven till all the water is drained up, add good milk or cream, a little salt when quite stiff beat it well with a spoon, let it be pretty stiff & put it in a mould, to turn out – garnish it with Marmalade or sweetmeat & pour over it coloured cream or custard.

> *Rice prepared in this way may be laid over fruits and baked instead of a Crust. It should be laid in separate spoonful & look broken.* [15]

> *2oz/50g short-grain rice*   *pinch of salt*
> *¼pt/150ml cream*

Put the rice in a baking dish, cover with ¾pt/450ml cold water, and bake at 150°C, 300°F, Gas Mark 2 for 30 min., stir, bake for a further 30 min., stir in the cream, and continue to bake for a further hour.

Remove from the oven, remove any skin, then sprinkle with the salt, and beat thoroughly. It may then be packed into a freshly-rinsed 1pt/600ml mould, and left in a cool place for a few hours to set. Turn out onto a dish and garnish with marmalade, jam, or preserved [tinned] fruit.

Pears were among the fruits which might be stewed from the raw to accompany the rice. This recipe states that they should be stewed for hours along with a new pewter spoon. This was a well-known method of turning the pears an attractive purple colour as they absorbed elements of the lead and tin components of the pewter released by the acids.[16] This practice should never be repeated today, the same effect being obtained from a few drops of modern food colouring.

Pears to stew

Pare the largest stewing pears & stick a clove into the blossom end then put them in a tin Pan with a new pewter spoon in the middle, fill it with hard water & set it over a slow fire for 3 or 4 Hours till soft & the water reduced to a small quantity. then put as much loaf sugar as will make it a thick syrup & let the pears boil in it, then cut lemon peel like straws & serve them up with the syrup in a glass dish [17]

6 cooking pears	1tsp purple food colour
6 cloves	pared zest of 1 lemon
6oz/150g sugar	

Peel the pears, stick a clove in the bottom of each one and stew with the sugar, food colour and sufficient water to just cover, for about 30 min. until tender. Strain the liquid into a clean pan and boil rapidly until reduced to half its volume, and leave to cool. Meanwhile slice the lemon zest into very fine straws and simmer in plain water for 5 min., drain, and rinse in cold water. Finally arrange the pears in a dish, pour the syrup over them, and sprinkle with the lemon straws.

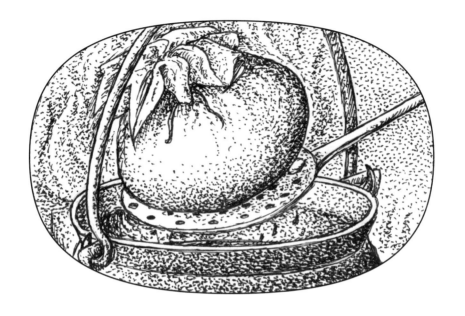

Chapter Five

OF HOT PUDDINGS
& SWEET PIES

Puddings are now thought of as being sweet dishes, but they originated as large savoury boiled sausages, including the black pudding, still an essential ingredient in any local breakfast or tatie-pot. By the Elizabethan period larger puddings became possible by enclosing ingredients in cloths, as well as prepared guts. Using combinations of flour, milk or cream and eggs, all mixed with various flavourings, very hot and satisfying puddings could now be made, ideal for providing substantial accompaniments to roast and stewed meats etc. It was only with the widespread use of potatoes to fulfil this role that the boiled pudding changed to an almost exclusively sweet dish. Around 1800 this change was actively taking place, and so recipe books still provided instructions for making unsweetened puddings either to accompany meats or to be served with a sweet white sauce. One of the most basic of these was the boiled batter pudding, Dorothy making a 'batter pudding for William' in May, 1802.[1] Since she did not record her own recipe, this example comes from a manuscript of around 1810 written in the North Yorkshire/County Durham area, which included the Hutchinsons' home at Sockburn.

Boiled Batter Pudding

Beat the Yolks of three Eggs with two large spoonfuls of Flour, a little Salt, a pint of good Milk or Cream, make it the thickness of a Pancake [batter], & beat all well together. An hour will boil it.

Mrs Bell Selaby.[2]

3 yolks of egg, beaten	*8oz/225g flour, sifted*
1pt/600ml milk or cream	*pinch of salt*

Beat the eggs into the milk or cream, then beat in the flour and salt until smooth and thick.

Take a double thickness of either very fine muslin or finely-woven cotton or linen, about 18ins/45cm square, soak it in boiling water, lightly wring it, shake out, lay on a flat surface, and smooth out any wrinkles. Sprinkle a thin layer of flour all over it, lift it up by the ends of one side, shake off any surplus flour, and lay inside a deep bowl, the edges overhanging the sides.

Half fill a large pan with water, and bring to a rapid boil. Pour the batter into the cloth, gather up the sides first, then the corners, until the batter is totally enclosed, and tie securely with string or twine. Immediately lift up the pudding and plunge it into the boiling water, using any long-handled utensil to turn it tied-side down, cover, return to the boil, and continue a strong simmer for 1½ hours, topping up with boiling water in order to keep the pudding floating.

When ready to serve, remove the pan from the heat, and scoop up the pudding in a strong wire sieve, or raise the corners of the cloth above the surface, and grasp either with strong tongs or with a double layer of thick towel, dip rapidly in and out of cold water in a basin just big enough to hold it, which will allow the cloth to be more easily untied, and the pudding turned out onto a hot dish.

Variations: add either 1-2 tsp ground ginger, or 1-2oz/25-50g currants, or 3-4tbs sugar to the batter.

Sauce: The usual sauce for puddings of this kind was made by melting together 4oz/100g each of butter, sugar and white wine.

On Christmas morning, 1805, young Johnny Wordsworth was 'alive at the thought of two plum-puddings which are now rumbling in the Pot.³ Unfortunately their recipe has not survived, this one coming from Martha Fricker:

To Make a Plum Pudding

1lb of Currants, half lb of Raisins chopped, half lb of Suet, the rind of a Lemon grated half an ounce of Canddid Lemon two Tablespoonful of Sugar 4 Eggs & three table spoonful of Brandy ⁴

1lb/450g currants	*grated zest of a lemon*
8oz/225g chopped raisins	*2tbs sugar*

8oz/225g suet	3tbs brandy
½oz/12g candied lemon peel	4 eggs, beaten
8oz/225g flour	

Mix the dry ingredients thoroughly, beat the eggs and brandy together, pour in and work together to form a uniformly stiff dough. Take a piece of fine cotton cloth or a doubled layer of muslin some 2ft/60cm square, scald, wring, spread out, and dust the top surface with flour. Shake off the surplus, lay across a bowl, and place the dough, formed into a ball, in the centre. Gather the cloth around it, centres of the sides first, and tie tightly with string.

Plunge into boiling water, cover, and continue at a strong simmer, topping up with more boiling water as necessary, for 4 hours. Scoop out of the pot with a strong wire sieve, place on a hot dish, remove the string, turn out of the cloth, and serve immediately.

Sometimes a plain pudding was required either at short notice, or when other demands left little time for the mixing, tying up and long period of boiling. Its place might then be taken by the appropriately-named Hasty Pudding, which Dorothy made for her supper after a busy day of gardening, walking and writing in May, 1800.[5] Since she used the word 'porridge' for its oatmeal equivalent, hers was most probably based on flour and milk.

Flour Hasty Pudding

Put four bay-leaves into a quart of milk, and set it on the fire to boil. Then beat up the yolks of two eggs, and stir in a little salt. Take two or three spoonfuls of milk, and beat up with your eggs, and stir in your milk. Then with a wooden spoon in one hand, and the flour in the other, stir it in till it be of a good thickness, but not too thick. Let it boil, and keep stirring; then pour it into a dish, and stick pieces of butter here and there. [6]

1 egg yolk	2oz/50g flour
pinch of salt	2 bayleaves
1pt/600ml milk	1oz/25g butter

97

Beat the yolk with a little of the milk, then add the remaining milk, salt and bayleaves, then sifting in the flour little by little while beating vigorously. Stir over a medium heat until it has boiled for 5 min., then pour it into a dish and dot with butter.

Some of the other boiled puddings were rather more delicate, Joanna Hutchinson's Custard Pudding, for example, being so lightly set with eggs that it tends to collapse into a mound when turned out onto its dish.

Custard Pudding

A pint of Good milk (better with some cream) 4 Eggs, a small spoonful of Flour, boil it 40 minutes; and hang it up ½ an hour at least. Put it in boiling water again for from 5 to 10 minutes [7]

½pt/300ml single cream	*4 eggs, beaten*
½pt/300ml milk	*3tbs flour*

Beat the cream, milk and eggs together, then sift in the flour while beating vigorously, then boil in a cloth, as described in the recipe for Boiled Batter Pudding above, removing it from the water after 40 min., hanging it up for 30 min. to cook through, and finally returning to boil for 10 min. just before serving.

Since this batter is quite thin, the initial plunge into hot water should be executed as quickly as possible. Alternatively pour it into a greased basin, cover with a piece of kitchen foil pressed over the rim, and steam instead of boiling.

One Sunday in early June, 1800, Dorothy 'walked up to Mr Simpson's to gather gooseberries it was a fine afternoon. Little Tommy [the son of a friend] came with me, ate gooseberry pudding and drank tea with me.'[8] We do not have her recipe, but it was probably similar to this one used by Rachel Whitwell of Kendal (1771-1833). It produces a very rich, moist and well-flavoured pudding, the gooseberries contributing their characteristic sharpness. It is useful in converting relatively few gooseberries into a very satisfying pudding. If a sauce is required, use double cream.

To make a boiled Gooseberry Pudding

6oz [150g] gooseberries	*3 Eggs (well beat)*
6oz [150g] grated bread	*Nutmeg [pinch]*
6oz [150g] Currants	*Lemon peel [grated zest]*
6oz [150g] Sugar	*a [table] spoon of Brandy*
1½ or 2 hours boiling [9]	

Pick the gooseberries, trim off the projecting stalks etc. and chop each in half. Place in a bowl with the remaining dry ingredients, mix thoroughly, then stir in the eggs and brandy. Boil, as described in the recipe for Boiled Batter Pudding, above, for 2 hours.

Boiled puddings were relatively economical to make, since they could be cooked over any open fire. Baked puddings, meanwhile, even though less troublesome, required extra fuel to heat up the traditional stone-built ovens. Most of their recipes were very similar to their boiled equivalents:

Baked Batter Pudding

Two Spoonfuls of Flour, 4 Yolk of Eggs, & 2 Whites, one Gill of Cream, mix the Eggs & Cream together, then add the Flour, beat them all well for five Minutes, then bake them in Tea Cups for 20 Minutes.

Mrs Blakey, Minsteracres[10]

Use the butter or dripping to grease the insides of six heatproof basins or large metal bun-tins, and arrange on a baking tray. Beat the yolks into the cream, then sift in the flour while beating vigorously, to make a thick batter. [if possible leave to rest for 30 60 min.] Pour the batter into the basins/tins, and bake at 170°C, 325°F, Gas mark 3 for 20 min.

German Puffs were a rather more sophisticated version. Originally made by dropping spoonfuls of sweet batter into a deep pan of boiling fat to emerge as plum-shaped fritters, by around 1800 they had become puddings baked in cups.

To make German Puffs

Take the yolks of four eggs, two spoonfuls of flour, two ounces of sweet almonds beat fine, mix them well together and then add to it a pint of thick cream, two ounces of butter clarified; When cold, put that in, and sugar to your taste, add a little orange flower water. Bake them in little pans well buttered, and in a quick oven. Twenty minutes will bake them Your sauce must be melted butter with white wine and sugar. [11]

2 egg yolks, beaten	*1oz/25g butter*
4oz/100g flour	*2oz/50g sugar*
1oz/25g ground almonds	*2tbs orange flower water*
½pt/300ml cream	
The Sauce:	
4oz/100g butter 4oz/100g sugar	*¼pt/150ml white wine*

Beat the flour and almonds into the yolks, with a little of the cream, until smooth, then beat in the rest of the cream. Melt the butter in a small pan, allow to cool, and beat the clear into the mixture, along with the sugar and orange flower water. Butter six plain bun-tins, pour in the mixture, and bake at 170°C, 325°F, Gas mark 3 for 20 min, then turn out on to hot plates.

Melt the sauce ingredients together, and pour over the puddings.

3 Puddings [Gooseberry, Apple, Apricot]

Upon 2 handfuls of bread crumbs pour a pint of Cream boiling hot, when cold add 5 Eggs well beaten and 4 spoonfuls of the pulp of scalded Gooseberries, Apples, or Apricots the rind of a Lemon, sugar to the Taste, a glass of white Wine, or a little Brandy paste the dish & bake it [12]

4oz/100g fresh white breadcrumbs	*8oz/225g flour*
grated zest of 1 lemon	*3tbs sugar*
1pt/600ml single cream	
1tbs white wine or 1 tbs brandy	
6oz/150g cooked apricot, apple or gooseberry, pulped	
4oz/100g butter, or half butter	

Bring the cream to the boil, in a saucepan, stirring to prevent it burning, remove from the heat as soon as it has risen to the boil, and stir in the breadcrumbs. Cover, and set aside to cool. Meanwhile use the flour and butter to make a short pastry (alternatively use 1lb/450g puff pastry) and use to line a 2pt/1·2l baking dish.

When the cream mixture is cool, beat in the fruit, eggs, sugar, lemon and wine or brandy, until smooth. Pour this into the pastry-lined dish and bake at 150°C, 300°F, Gas mark 2 for 1½ hours until risen and just browning around the edges.

Earthenware baking dishes had been manufactured by most of the large pottery factories from the late eighteenth century. Relatively cheap to buy, they enabled 'pudding-pies' to be baked either without the necessity of raising a free-standing hot-water crust, or of providing any bottom crust at all. One of these 'bakers' was probably in use at the King's Head at Thirlspot a few days after Christmas, 1801. Here, after crossing Dunmail Raise on their way to visit Coleridge in Keswick, William, Mary and Dorothy 'roasted apples in the oven.'[13]

Roasted Apples

1 medium cooking apple per person

Wipe and core each apple, and make a shallow cut through the skin all around its middle. Place on a baking dish, and bake at 200°C, 400°F, Gas mark 6 for about 40-60 min until soft. The Wordsworths' apples were probably baked in this way, but alternatively their centres may be stuffed with sugar and a knob of butter, with chopped dried and glacé fruits, or with mincemeat (*see p103*) before going into the oven.

Baking dishes were also useful for baking milk puddings, many of which were considered as much as invalid foods as puddings. This is certainly the impression given by Dorothy's decision 'to take Tapioca for my supper' in January 1803.[14] Mary's use of a stiff rice pudding to form the crust of a baked apple pie is both an interesting and a successful combination. The distinctive flavours and textures of the rice and apple complement each other ideally, and are an improvement on the usual shortcrust pastry. [15]

Rice [& Fruit Pie]

Rice prepared as in the recipe on p.126
1½lb/675g sliced apple or other raw fruit
2oz/50g sugar, pinch ground cinnamon

Arrange the fruit in the bottom of a baking dish about
6 x 8ins/15 x 20cm, sprinkling it with the sugar and
cinnamon. Drop rough spoonfuls of the cooked rice on top
to cover the fruit, and bake at 180°C, 350°F, Gas mark 4 for
30 min. until the top is lightly browned, and serve either
hot or cold.

Dorothy's journal tells of the apple pies, gooseberry pies, apple tarts,
and rhubarb tarts which she baked at Dove Cottage.[16] These were most
probably simply made with shortcrust pastry, rather than the more
elaborate puff-paste versions given in the published recipe books of the
period. The prepared fruit would have been arranged in the baking
dishes or in pastry-lined tart tins, sprinkled with sugar, perhaps with
grated lemon zest, ground clove or cinnamon as appropriate, covered
with an upper crust if intended for a pie, and baked in the oven.

When William, Mary and Dorothy Wordsworth called at the
King's Head. Thirlspot, on 28th December, 1801, they found John
Stanley's family making Christmas Pies.[17] The following day, as they
approached Ullswater, they 'dined at the publick house on porridge,
with a second course of Christmas pies'. At this time a Christmas Pie
could take a number of forms, anything from a giant pie filled with
all manner of poultry and gamebirds stuffed one within another, and
weighing a stone or two, as in Yorkshire, to the equivalent of a modern
meatless mince pie. The nature of the Lake District Christmas Pie in
the eighteenth century was fortunately described in a letter sent by 'A
Gentleman of Cumberland' to Richard Bradley, Professor of Botany at
Cambridge University, who published it in 1732. Describing the local
sweet haggis, called a hackin, he stated 'that it eats somewhat like a
Christmas Pye, or is somewhat like that boil'd'.[18] Since its ingredients
included minced lean beef, suet, shredded apples, currants, lemon
peel and sugar, it was obviously a sweet minced pie, a forerunner
of the traditional Cumbrian 'Sweet Pie'. This recipe, collected by
Rachel Whitwell of Kendall (1771–1833) is much pleasanter, lighter and
sharper than most modern mincemeats.

Fig 11. The late eighteenth century creamware potteries made wares ideal for baking pies, including bakers (top) which only required a top crust, patty pans (centre) and plates (bottom).

Mrs Mathew's Recipt for Minc'd pies

Two pounds [900g] of Beef Suet Shred fine, three pounds [1·8kg] of baking Apples, the Peel of a Lemon Shred Small, one pound & half [675g] of Sugar, two ditto currants, half a pound [225g] of Raisins, a quarter of a pound [100g] of Citron, a quarter [100g] of Lemon & orange peel, the juice of two or three Lemons, half a pint [300ml] of Brandy, an Ounce [25g] of Cinnamon, one Nutmeg, and a quarter of a pound [100g] of Almonds. [19]

Mix all the ingredients together (the quantity of suet has been halved to suit modern taste), press down into jars and seal, store in a cool place, and use within a month. Make up the plate or individual pies with either shortcrust or puff pastry, and bake at 220°C, 425°F, Gas mark 7 for about 20 min.

The final recipe in this chapter is for Raspberry Fritters, a useful addition to the dining table, especially for those dull, wet summer evenings so often experienced in the Lake District.

Raspberry Fritters

Pour ½ Gill of boiling cream upon some bread crumbs, beat the yolks of 4 Eggs to a froth, when the cream &c. is cold beat it a little then put all together very much & add 2oz of sugar & as much of the juice of Raspberries as will make it a pretty colour & give it an agreeable sharpness. drop them into a pan of boiling Lard the size of a Walnut. [20]

4oz/100g raspberries	*2oz/50g sugar*
5oz/125g fresh white breadcrumbs	*4 egg yolks*
⅛pt/75ml cream	*lard for frying*

Place the raspberries in a sieve over a jug, crush with a fork, and then use either the back of a spoon or the fingertips to press through all the juice.

Mix the bread and sugar in a bowl, pour on the cream heated to boiling, and stir in with a fork until completely incorporated, then leave to cool for 10 min. before stirring in the raspberry juice. Whisk the yolks until they are transformed into a pale yellow froth, and finally fold them into the mixture.

Heat a pan with sufficient lard [or oil] for deep-frying, using the lowest setting if using a deep-fryer. Using two dessert spoons, scoop up walnut-sized pieces of the mixture, and rapidly drop a number of these into the hot lard. They will sink at first, and may stick to the bottom unless eased off with a metal slice. When they have risen to the surface and their undersides are pale golden brown, checked by turning over, turn them all over to cook on the other side, then remove onto paper towels to drain, and keep hot while frying succeeding batches. Serve piping hot and sprinkled with sugar. N.B. If fried at too high a temperature, the outsides will be overcooked to dark brown while the insides are still virtually raw.

Chapter Six

OF BREAD & CAKES

D orothy Wordsworth's Grasmere journal records her frequent baking sessions at Dove Cottage but, even though they might take place at roughly weekly intervals, no particular day of the week was selected for a baking day, as was customary in households with more regular domestic timetables. The oven at Dove Cottage was almost certainly of the traditional 'beehive' design, a domed masonry chamber a few feet in diameter built into the back kitchen chimney stack. Its only opening would have been a square doorway roughly at table height, into which were thrust bound bundles of small branches called faggots. William and Dorothy made one of these from trees blown down from 'John's Grove' after a storm in January 1802.[1] Having been ignited and pushed to the back of the oven, their flames roared against the domed roof, heating the masonry before emerging from the upper part of the doorway and escaping up the chimney. When sufficiently hot, the embers were raked out onto the hearth, the ashes swept out with a wet mop called a fruggan, the bakery inserted, and the door closed for the required cooking time. The efficient management of such ovens required considerable practical experience, but within a few months of arriving at Dove Cottage Dorothy had deputised much of this responsibility on to her neighbour and servant Molly Fisher. Writing to Jane Pollard in September 1800, she described how Molly 'looks to the oven', while in June 1802 she was able to tell Sara Hutchinson that 'Molly manages the oven entirely and as well as I can'.[2] Even so, Molly's opinions could still lead to absolute disaster. In May 1802 William explained to Coleridge the reasons why Dorothy would not be sending him his promised supper-cake: 'it died of a very common malady, bad advice. The oven must be hot, perfectly hot, said Molly the experienced, so in a piping red-hot oven it went, and came out (but I hate antithesis) in colours especially black as a genuine child of the coal-hole. In plain English, it is not a sendable article.'[3]

In the same letter he described Dorothy 'packing up a few small loaves of American flour'. These, being of hard or strong wheat, would have been lighter and spongier than those made from the traditional soft English wheats. Since dried forms of bread-yeasts had still to be developed, all bakers, whether working on a commercial or domestic scale, used ale-yeasts, sour-dough or home-made yeasts to raise their doughs. Dorothy appears to have changed to making home-made yeasts before 1802, when she told Sara Hutchinson that 'I am glad you found out how to bake bread in my way – we never want yeast now.'[4] Her method may have been either of the following, noted by Joanna Hutchinson:

To make Yeast

One Gallon of water, one ounce Hops 2 pounds flower, boil the hops 20 minutes then have your potatoes bruised small, then stir in the above quantity of flower, [min?] altogether with the liquor. when less than new Milk warm add 1 quart of old yeast to it & let it stand all night, it may be used in the morning, great nicety must be used to keep the stone bottles sweet it is kept in, the hops should be strained before they are mixed (boiling hot). you may omit the potatoes if you like [5]

Yeast

Boil 1oz of hops about 10 minutes in 6 quarts of water, strain it and mix it immediately with 2lbs of flour and a tablespoonful of sugar, when the mixture is new milk warm add two spoonfuls of good yeast, put it in a stone bottle, cork it well and in two days it will be fit for use, half this quantity is sufficient for about 2 pecks of flour.

Reserve ½ a pint to make the yeast the next time. The night before you bake put a quart to a portion of the flour mixed then, in the morning knead it and bake in the afternoon.[6]

Joanna also obtained another recipe from a Mrs King:

Potatoe Yeast

Boil mealy Potatoes till quite soft, skin & mash them very smooth & put as much hot water as will make them the consistence of common Yeast. Add to every 1lb of Potatoes 2oz of coarse sugar, & when just warm stir into every lb of Potatoes 2 spoonful of common yeast & keep it till it has done fermenting & in 24 hours it may be used. 1lb of potatoes will make a quart of yeast & when made it will keep 3 months. Make the Dough 8 hours before it is to be baked.

Mrs King [7]

Fig 12. This drawing after John Harden of Brathay shows a middle-class lady instructing her servant in 1804. Their contrasting status is clearly defined by their respective poses and dress, almost as if depicting Dorothy instructing Old Molly Fisher at Dove Cottage in 1800.

As these recipes show, it was customary to start the bread-making process the previous night or at least eight hours before baking. The liquid yeast was mixed with sufficient flour to form a soft batter, which was then covered with more flour and allowed to ferment slowly. The rest of the flour was then kneaded into this 'sponge' and left to rise in the usual way. This method ensured that the bread was always well-risen and well-flavoured when it emerged from the oven. It was then ready for consumption either as bread and butter, toast, or as breadcrumbs in puddings, forcemeats and sauces.

This recipe from the Frícker recipe book shows how yeasted dough was used to make either rich caraway buns or hot cross buns:

To make light Barm [Buns & Hot Cross Buns]

Take 2 pounds & a half of Flour – rub into it ½ pound of sugar & some pounded Caraway seeds– mix 8 table spoonfuls of light barm with 6 eggs well beaten & rather more than ½ pint of warm milk. Make a hole in the Flour & pour in the liquid – cover it & set it by the fire for 2 hours to rise – make the buns up with as little Flour as possible – bake them in a quick oven
N.B. if you want them for Good Friday, add a few Cloves, a little Mace & Cinnamon beaten & sifted – and cross them.[8]

1lb/450g strong white flour	*3oz/75g sugar*
3oz/75g butter	*¼pt/150ml tepid milk*
1tbs caraway seeds	*2 eggs, beaten*
1tbs dried yeast	

Follow the manufacturer's instructions for the dried yeast, either activating it with 1tsp of sugar and a little of the tepid milk whisked together and left in a warm place for about 20 min. until frothy, before adding with the milk, or add the dried yeast with the caraway seeds etc.

Rub the butter into the flour, mix in the caraway seeds and sugar, make a well in the centre, pour in the tepid milk and eggs, and work together to form a dough. Knead on a floured board for 5 min. then place in a bowl, cover with a cloth and leave in a warm place to rise until doubled in size. Divide into 12 pieces, mould into round buns, place on a lightly greased baking sheet, a few inches apart, cover again, and return to the warm until doubled in size, then bake at 190°C, 375°F, Gas mark 5 for 15-20min., until golden brown.

For Hot Cross buns, add ½tsp each of ground clove, mace and cinnamon instead of the caraway seeds, slash their tops with a cross as soon as moulded into buns and brush over with 4tbs milk and water, and 3tbs sugar melted together just as they come out of the oven.

Martha Fricker also made this fruit loaf, which was made up and baked in the same way:

A Bun Loaf

½lb Raisins	½ [lb] Sugar
½lb Currants	two Eggs
½lb Butter	a little Nutmeg & Barm
2lb Flour	
To rise an hour [9]	

Some fruit cakes were also yeast-raised, just like modern plum-loaves, while others were raised either by a combination of yeast and eggs, or by eggs alone. A Fricker recipe advised that:

Whether black or white Plum cakes they require less butter and eggs for having yeast, and equally light and rich. If the leaven [yeast] be only of flour, milk and water and yeast, it becomes tough & is less easily divided than if the butter be first put with these ingredients & the dough afterwards set to rise before the fire.[10]

For these, as well as the lighter egg-raised cakes, the Frickers wrote down their:

Observations on making and baking Cakes

Currants should be very nicely washed, dried in a Cloth and then set before the fire. If damp they will make Cakes or puddings heavy. Before they are added a dust of dry flour should be thrown among them, and a shake given to them which causes the thing to which they are put to be lighter.

Eggs should be very long beaten, whites and yolks apart and always strained.

Sugar should be rubbed to a powder on a clean board and sifted through a very fine hair or lawn sieve.

Lemon-peel should be pared very thin, and with a little sugar beaten in a marble mortar to a paste, and then mixed with a little wine or cream, so as to divide easily among the other ingredients.

After all the ingredients are put into the pan they should be thoroughly and long beaten as the lightness of the Cake depends much on these being well incorporated ...

The heat of the oven is of great importance for Cakes, especially larger ones – if not quick their batter will not rise, but some paper should be put over the Cake to prevent it being burnt. If not long enough lighted to have a body of heat or it is become slack, the cake will be heavy.

To know when it is soaked take a broad-bladed knife that is very bright and plunge it into the very centre [of the cake], draw it instantly out, and if the least stickiness adheres put the cake immediately in and shut up the oven.

If the heat should be sufficient to raise but not to soak, fresh fuel might be quickly put in & the Cake kept hot until the oven was fit to finish the soaking – but great care should be taken that no mistakes occur from negligence in baking large cakes. [11]

Using this advice the Frickers were able to make rich fruit cakes such as this:

Plum Cake

lb of Raisins 2lb Currants ½lb Citron ½ of Lemon 1(?)lb of Flour 1lb½ Sugar 2 Nutmegs 1lb of Eggs (10) a Wine Glass of Brandy Dº of Port wine 1lb & ¼ of butter without salt
beat the butter to a Cream then add the yolks of the eggs – then the whites well beaten – then all the other ingredients by degrees, except the Lemon, & Citron which are stuck upright between the layers of Cake in the dish – bake it in a moderate oven about 5 hours & ½ [12]

1lb/450g raisins	*8 eggs, separated*
2lb/900g currants	*3tbs brandy*
8oz/225g candied peel	*3tbs port*
8oz/225g citron, chopped	*2 nutmegs, grated*
1lb 4oz/550g butter	*1lb/450g flour*
1lb 8oz/675g sugar	

Line a 9ins/23cm square or 10ins/25.5cm round tin with buttered paper. Mix the currants and raisins, and the candied peel and citron.

The original recipe makes it difficult to prevent the butter from separating from the mixture, and so the following version adopts the usual modern method.

Cream the butter with the sugar, and work in, little by little, the beaten yolks, the whites whipped to a soft peak, and the brandy and port. Fold in the flour sifted with the nutmeg, and then the raisins and currants. Spread a third of the mixture into the tin, scatter on half of the candied peel and citron, then another third of the mixture, the rest of the peel and citron, and finally the remaining mixture. Bake at 150°C, 300°F, Gas mark 2 for 5½ hours, covering the top with paper after the first hour.

Icing for the Plumb Cake

ice it when nearly cold, rubbing it with flour first, the bottom is to be iced not the top.[13]

If intended for use as a bride-cake, as wedding cakes were then known, the cake was sometimes given a preliminary coat of almond paste (some 2lb 4oz/1kg for one of this size). Others had the icing laid directly on to their baked surfaces. This was made by whisking the whites of four small eggs to each pound/450g of icing sugar until they formed a thick cream which was applied using a flat spoon.

Most of the more delicate cakes of this period were variations of the fatless sponge, which relied on beating or whisking very fresh egg yolks and whites, then mixing in sugar, flour and some form of flavouring before baking in a cool or moderate oven. If skilfully made they were amazingly light and spongy, with a crisp crust and a sweet eggy flavour, absolutely ideal to enjoy fresh with either a cup of tea or a glass of wine. If hurriedly made, with insufficient beating, they failed to rise, and their sponge became decidedly chewy. Reputations were made or broken on the respective quality of a person's sponge cakes, so long as the tradition of home baking flourished in England.

White Cakes

*1lb of Butter beaten to a cream, 9 Eggs leaving out the white of 3,
1lb of Flour well dried – 1lb of loaf sugar beat & sifted – the rind
of a Lemon grated (also the juice when it is put into the the oven)
¼lb candied Lemon – 2oz of sweet & 2oz of bitter almonds. By
adding ¼ of currants it will be an excellent 'fruit' cake.* [14]

grated zest & juice of 1 lemon	*6oz/150g butter*
2oz/50g candied lemon peel	*6oz/150g sugar*
2oz/50g ground almonds	*3 eggs, beaten*
6oz/150g flour	*1tsp almond essence*
2oz/50g currants – optional	

Beat the butter to a cream, beat in the sugar until white and
fluffy, then the eggs, little by little, and finally the lemon
zest, lemon peel, almonds and, if chosen, the currants.

Line a 7ins/18cm cake tin with non-stick baking
parchment, put in the mixture, levelling the top, and bake at
180°C, 350°F, Gas mark 4 for around 1 hour.

In the next recipe ground rice provides a pleasantly gritty texture,
being an early version of the popular Victorian sand-cakes. It was
considered to be an excellent cake for making trifles.

Rice Cake

*15 Eggs leaving out 7 whites beat them well for an hour – add by
degrees 1lb of loaf sugar beat & sifted with ½lb ground rice – beat
in ¼ of an hour longer – butter the pan & bake it in a quick oven
– don't fill the pan too full.* [15]

6 eggs, less 3 whites	*4oz/150g ground rice*
6oz/150g caster sugar	

Line a 7ins/18cm cake tin with greaseproof paper, brush
the inside with melted butter, and dust with a mixture of
flour and caster sugar.

Beat the eggs until almost white, then beat in the sugar
little by little, and finally the rice. Continue beating/
whisking for 10 minutes, until the mixture is pale and

foamy, then pour into the lined tin and place immediately into the oven pre-heated to 180°C, 350°F, Gas mark 4, baking it for 45 min. Allow to cool a little, and then remove the tin etc.

'Diet cakes' were very light cakes, suitable for delicate digestions, but their eggs and sugar were unlikely to encourage a loss of weight. Other contemporary versions suggest that either a little sugar should be sprinkled over them just before going into the oven, or that they should be iced when cold.[16]

Diet Bread Cake

Take a large Lemon & grate it into the yolks of seven Eggs ½lb of loaf sugar grated 4 whites of Eggs – beat the remainder for 20 minutes Stir in gently ½lb of flour bake it in a slow oven for ½ an hour – The yolks & whites must be beaten separate [17]

grated zest of a lemon	4oz/100g caster sugar
4 yolks & 2 whites of eggs	4oz/100g flour

Line a 7ins/18cm cake tin with buttered paper. Beat the yolks and sugar together for 10 min. until light and creamy. Beat the whites separately to a soft peak, and fold them into the yolks with the lemon zest. Sift the flour into the mixture, little by little, gently folding it in to form a smooth, light mixture. Pour this into the prepared cake tin, and bake at 150°C, 300°F, Gas mark 2 for some 40 min. until the top is a deep cream colour.

In March 1802 Dorothy Wordsworth baked a seedcake for her friend Mr.Simpson.[18] The distinctive flavour of caraway was greatly appreciated at this period, especially in sponge cakes enriched with butter, as in this recipe from Mrs Elizabeth Raffald of Manchester's *Experienced English Housekeeper* of 1769.

To make a rich Seed Cake

Take a pound of flour well dried, a pound of butter, a pound of loaf sugar beat and sifted, eight eggs, two ounces of carraway seeds, one nutmeg grated and its weight of cinnamon. First beat your butter to a cream, then put in your sugar. Beat the whites of your eggs half an hour, mix them with your sugar and butter. Then beat the yolks half an hour, put it to the whites, beat in your flour, spices and seeds a little before it goes to the oven. Put it in the hoop and bake for two hours in a quick oven and let it stand two hours. It will take two hours beating.[19]

8oz/225g plain flour	*8oz/225g butter*
1tsp grated nutmeg	*8oz/225g caster sugar*
1tsp ground cinnamon	*4 eggs, separated*
1oz/25g caraway seeds	

Line an 8ins/20cm cake tin with buttered paper. Beat the yolks until light and creamy, and the whites to a soft peak. Cream the butter with the sugar, fold in the whites, then the yolks, sprinkle in the caraway seeds and finally shake in the flour and spices little by little through a sieve, folding in to produce a soft mixture. Turn into the tin, and bake at 170°C, 325°F, Gas mark 3 for 1½ hours.

In the eighteenth century the word 'biscuit' was used not only for what we recognise as biscuits today, but also for what Americans now call cup-cakes or muffins. Some were baked in hand-pleated paper cases, while others went into 'pans', deep tart-tins made of either tinplate or salt-glazed stoneware.

Satin Biscuits [small cakes]

The yolks of 12 & the whites of 2 Eggs, beat them well with 2 spoonfuls of Rose water put them in a pound of loaf sugar beaten. stir it well – then add ¾lb flour well dried butter the pans & fill them ½ full.[20]

5 yolks and 1 white of fresh eggs	*8oz/225g caster sugar*
1tbs rosewater	*6oz/150g flour*

Butter a number of bun-tins, and dust with a mixture of caster sugar and flour. Beat the yolks, white and rosewater together, then gradually beat in the sugar, and continue beating until the mixture is very light, before folding in the flour very gently. Half-fill the bun-tins, and bake at 180°C, 350°F, Gas mark 4 for some 30 minutes.

Queen cakes were similar, but were baked in 'small saucers or fluted tins made for this purpose' or heart shaped tins.[21]

Queen Cakes

8 Eggs – 1lb loaf Sugar beat & sifted, whisk these together ½ an hour then add 1lb of flour dried 1lb of Butter beat smooth mix all together ½ an hour longer, Either put Currants, ½lb or Almonds & Candied Lemon, with a glass of brandy.[22]

2 eggs, beaten	2oz/50g currants or 2oz/50g
4oz/100g butter	ground almonds & candied peel
4oz/100g caster sugar	
4oz/100g flour 1tbs brandy	

Prepare a number of small bun-tins, about 2ins/5cm diameter, by brushing their interiors with melted butter and dusting them with a mixture of flour and caster sugar, knocking to remove the surplus.

Beat the eggs until they are in a pale, creamy state, fold in half the flour, then the butter beaten and warmed until semi-liquid, and finally the remaining flour and ingredients. Half-fill the pans and bake at 180°C, 350°F, Gas mark 4 for 20-25 minutes, allow to cool a little, then invert and tap, when they should fall free.

It is rather surprising to find instructions for jumbles in Joanna Hutchinson's recipe book, since these knotted biscuits originated as part of the sweetmeat banquet fare offered at well-to-do Elizabethan entertainments.

Jumballs

¼lb Butter beat to a cream ½lb flour dried ½lb loaf sugar beat & sifted, the rind of a lemon grated – a spoonful of Rose water–mix all together & make it into a paste with 2 Eggs – leave a little of the flour to make up the Cakes – let it stand 2 hours till stiff then make them up & bake them.[23]

2oz/50g butter	1½tsp rosewater
4oz/100g sugar	grated zest of ½ a lemon
1 egg, beaten	5oz/150g flour

Cream the butter with the sugar, then beat in the egg, rosewater and lemon zest, little by little, to form a smooth mixture, then fold in the sifted flour, little by little, and finally knead to make a soft dough. Set aside for 2 hours to firm up, then divide into pieces, roll out on a floured board to about ¾ins/2cm diameter and form into rings, knots (like pretzels), plaits etc. Place on a lightly greased baking sheet and bake at 180°C, 350°F, Gas mark 4 for 15-20 min.

In the late eighteenth and early nineteenth centuries macaroons had to be made from almonds still in their shells. Having been cracked open, their kernels were plunged into boiling water and allowed to cool, enabling their brown skins to be pinched off, and moistening their insides. After a preliminary chopping, they were ground in a mortar, great care having to be taken to ensure that their oil was not squeezed out, since this transformed them into an irrecoverable oily mass. Only when reduced to a smooth, stiff paste could they be used for marzipans or in bakery mixtures. Today it is far easier to use ground almonds instead.

Macaroons

To 1lb of blanched & beaten sweet Almonds put one lb. of sugar & a little rosewater then beat the white of 7 Eggs to a froth put them in & beat all well together drop it on wafer papers grate sugar over & bake them.[24]

5oz/150g ground almonds	1tbs rosewater
5oz/150g caster sugar	2 whites of fresh eggs

Mix the almonds, sugar and rosewater in a basin. Using another bowl, whisk the egg whites to stiffness then add the almonds etc. and fold all together to form a soft mixture. Using a teaspoon, scoop up portions and use the index finger to push them off onto a piece of rice paper (or baking parchment), leaving at least 1ins/2·5cm between each one.

Bake at 180°C, 350°F, Gas mark 4 for 20-25 min. until golden brown.

The final recipe for egg-raised cakes is for the lightest and most delicate of them all, meringues. It comes from the Frickers, being distinctly high-quality confectionery in comparison to the sound, though excellent, cakes and biscuits of the Hutchinsons.

Meranghes

Whisk the whites of nine Eggs to the rind of 6 lemons and a spoonful of Sugar to be put on a tin prepared for them, sift sugar over them and be very quick to put them in the oven, bake in a moderate oven, dry them on a dish before the fire, turning them first. Put sweetmeats between two.[25]

> *3 medium sized fresh organic egg whites*
> *6oz/150g caster sugar*   *grated zest of 2 lemons*

Grease 2 baking sheets or cover with non-stick parchment. Whisk the eggs until stiff, then whisk in half the sugar little by little, and then gently fold in the remaining sugar mixed with the lemon zest. Drop tablespoons of the mixture onto the baking trays, leaving a space of at least 1½ ins/4cm between each one, and lightly sprinkle with caster sugar.

Bake at 110°C, 225°F, Gas mark ¼ for about 2½ 3 hours, until firm and crisp, but not browned, then cool on a wire rack.

Just before serving stick the flat side of each pair together with a little sharply-flavoured fruit jam.

The word 'gingerbread' covers a number of quite different items of bakery, everything from a spongy ginger cake to a semi-hard semispherical 'nut', a crisp biscuit or 'snap', a 'brandy-snap', a moulded cake-cum-biscuit covered in gilt foil, or a small round cake baked in a tin and called a 'pigginbottom'. Barbara Grey's shop in Kendal stocked a number of these, her celebrated products including:

> 'Her pigginbottoms, her brandysnaps,
> Her gingerbread cocks an' hens,
> An' men o' horseback decked i' gould
> They haa n't yan yet, by jems! &
> We nivver sall see sic a seet again
> As t' windo' at Barbr'y Gray's'.[26]

Fig 13. Barbara Grey's shop in Kendal stocked 'pigginbottoms' or spiced cakes baked in small tins, brandysnaps, and gingerbreads moulded as cocks and hens, and as men on horseback covered in gilt foil.

The Wordsworths bought their gingerbreads from Matthew Newton, 'the Blind Man', who earned his living by selling plants etc. In January 1803 Dorothy recorded how 'Wm had a fancy for some ginger bread. I put on Molly's Cloak and my Spenser and we walked towards Matthew Newton's. I went into the house. The blind Man and his Wife and Sister were sitting by the fire, all dressed very clean in their Sunday's Clothes, the sister reading. They took their little stock of gingerbread out of the cupboard and I bought 6 pennyworth. They were so grateful when I paid them for it that I could not find it in my heart to tell them we were going to make Gingerbread ourselves. I asked them if they had any thick 'No' answered Matthew 'there was none on Friday but we'll endeavour to get some.' The next Day the woman came just as we were baking and we brought 2 pennyworth.' [27] The thick gingerbread they were about to bake may have followed the usual form of 'block gingerbread' made throughout the northern counties, the following version being found in the recipe book of Rachel Whitwell of Kendal (1793-1833).

Gingerbread

*Flour & Treacle of each ¼St ½ Gill Brandy ½oz Carraway Seeds.
Do Clove Pepper, Do Ginger 2oz Butter 2oz Candied Lemon
½oz Pearl Ashes will be useful in making it rise* [28]

1lb/450g flour	*3tbs brandy*
½oz/12g candied peel	*1lb/450g black treacle*
1tsp bicarbonate of soda	*½oz/12g butter*
1½tsp each caraway seeds, ground ginger & allspice	

Line a loaf tin, or a 5ins/13cm square tin, with buttered paper. Sift together the flour, spices and soda, rub in the butter, add the peel, make a well in the centre, pour the warmed treacle in the middle, with the brandy, mix together, then knead until it is of an even colour. Pack into the prepared tin, level the top, and bake at 140°C, 275°F, Gas mark 1 for 2½ hours.

Both this and the next gingerbread emerge from the oven with the hardness and density of a house-brick. They should be wrapped in greaseproof paper and stored for a month or two in a cold slightly damp larder or cellar to mature and soften, and then sliced thinly and served with a good white cheese, such as Wensleydale or creamy or crumbly Lancashire.

Joanna Hutchinson's gingerbread has a lighter texture, provided by the use of eggs, sugar and more butter:

Joanna Hutchinson's Ginger bread

4lb Flour 2lb coarse sugar dried by the fire, 2lb of butter melted in 2lb of Treacle, mix two eggs well beaten with 2 spoonfuls of Brandy, put it into a dish & stir in the flour & sugar with some beat Ginger beat it at least an hour or till it comes clear from the bottom of the dish then set it by the fire till it is hot make it into cakes & bake it upon untin'd papers, or tin sheets Dry a qr. of a pound more flour to make the cakes up with. [29]

8oz/225g black treacle
8oz/225g butter
2tbs beaten egg
1½tsp brandy

1lb/450g flour
8oz/225g Demarara sugar
3tbs ground ginger

Warm the treacle and butter in a large pan (or microwave in a ceramic bowl for 30 seconds) and stir together until blended, then mix in the egg and brandy. Work in the dry ingredients, until they form a mass of soft dough which does not stick to the sides. At modern room temperature this takes a few minutes, certainly not an hour.

Either weigh in 4oz/100g pieces, roll between the palms to form a ball, place three inches apart on a baking sheet, and bake at 150°C, 300°F, Gas mark 2 for 50 minutes, or pack 1ins/2·5cm deep in lined loaf or cake tins, and bake at the same temperature for 1½ hours.

Martha Fricker's recipe is also of the lighter variety, using 'Salts Tartar' as a raising agent, in addition to eggs, to give a rather more open and cake-like texture.

Receipt for Gingerbread

1¾lb Flour 1lb Treacle¼lb Butter1d pennyworth Ginger
1 Do Carraway Seeds half a pennyworth of Salts Tartar ¼lb
Brown Sugar 2 Eggs & if too stiff add 2 Tablespoonful of Milk.
Mix up well together & put into a tin
 The Butter & Treacle put into a Jug and put into the oven until quite dissolved, stiring it occasionally [30]

12oz/350g flour
2tbs ground ginger
1tbs caraway seeds
2tsp cream of tartar
2oz/50g brown sugar

8oz/225g black treacle
2oz/50g butter
1 egg, beaten
2tbs milk

Line a loaf tin, or a 5ins/13cm square tin, with buttered paper. Mix all the dry ingredients in a bowl, and make a well in the centre. Place a small saucepan on the scales, weigh in the treacle, add the butter and stir over a gentle heat until combined. Allow to cool a little, then beat in the egg, pour the mixture into the bowl, and work in the flour etc. from the sides to form a dough, mixing in the milk to give a thick dropping consistency.

Pack into the prepared tin, level the top, and bake at 150°C, 300°F, Gas mark 2 for 1½ hours.

Gingerbread 'snaps' have to be kept perfectly dry in order to retain their essential crisp hardness. It is wise to try nibbling them before attempting a full bite, for they are far more solid than any modern ginger biscuit, but make up for this by having a richer flavour.

Gingerbread Snaps

Take 1 pound and half of Flour, and rub in ½ pound of Butter, one pound of coarse sugar & one ounce of Ginger beaten and sifted, mix the whole with 18 ounces of cold Treacle and a little Brandy – The Snaps will keep crisp any length of time in a Canister closely covered. [31]

12oz/350g flour	*2tbs ground ginger*
4oz/100g butter	*9oz/250g black treacle*
8oz/225g Demarara sugar	*1tbs brandy*

Rub the butter into the flour, mix in the sugar and ginger, make a well in the centre and pour in the treacle and brandy. Slip the hands into the flour beneath the treacle, and work the treacle into it, keeping the hands as free from the treacle as possible until all is combined into a firm even-coloured dough.

Roll out just over ⅛ins/·3cm thick, cut in 2-3ins/5-7·5cm rounds, and bake on greased baking sheets at 180°C, 350°F, Gas mark 4 for 20 minutes. Allow to cool before removing from the sheets.

Gingerbread [Snaps]

1½lb Treacle ½lb Sugar 9oz Butter Ginger to your taste A few cloves & a little lemon skin Rub the butter in as much flour as will make the paste stiff adding flour till it is so when you knead it. when the butter & treacle are stiff with cold put them within the air of the fire to soften. in warm weather this is not necessary. [32]

Gingerbread [Snaps] continued

12oz/350g flour	*12oz/350g black treacle*
4oz/100g butter	*2tbs ground ginger*
4oz/100g sugar	*¼tsp ground cloves*
grated rind of a lemon	

Make up and bake as for the previous recipe.

Gingerbread nuts, sometimes called hunting nuts since a number could be readily thrust into the pocket of a hunting jacket and eaten during the chase, were a rather more elegant form. The Frickers' recipe produces a much more open texture than any of the others reproduced here.

Gingerbread Nuts

Take 3 pounds of Flour, 1 pound of sugar, 1 pound &¼ of Butter, rubbed in very fine a large nutmeg grated 1oz &¾ of ginger, 2oz. of Carraway seeds, a few cloves, and a little mace and cinnamon beaten and sifted the rind of a large lemon grated mix all with the Flour melt a pint of Treacle with ¼ a pint of cream pour it into the Flour, & make it into a paste bake the nuts on Tin plates in a slack oven. [33]

12oz/350g flour	*¼tsp ground clove*
4oz/100g sugar	*¼tsp ground mace*
5oz/125g butter	*¼tsp ground cinnamon*
¼tsp grated nutmeg	*grated rind of a lemon*
4tsp ground ginger	*1lb/450g black treacle*
5tsp caraway seed	*tbs cream*

Rub the butter into the flour, and thoroughly mix in the dry ingredients. Just melt the treacle and cream together, without over-heating, and pour into a well in the flour etc. Mix in the flour from the sides until all is incorporated into a soft dough.

Lightly grease baking sheets, scoop up portions of the dough with a spoon, roll between the palms to form 1ins/2·5cm balls, and drop them on the sheets leaving about 1ins/2·5cm between each one. Bake at 180°C, 350°F, Gas

Above: Pace Eggs by James Dixon, general handyman, gardener and butler to the Wordsworths at Rydal Mount.

Below: Pages from Joanna Hutchinson's recipe book.

Top Left: A traditional char pot. Potted in such jars, the local fish were despatched in quantity to distant markets.

Top Right: The Wordsworths were used to fine tea-wares; Dorothy's cup and saucer survive in the collection at Dove Cottage.

Left: Wordsworth's "bait" tin contained the poet's sandwiches on fishing days.

Above: Jellies were always popular. Here, clockwise from the left, are a Madeira calf's foot jelly, a blancmange, a jaune mange, stone cream, orange jelly and strengthening jellies, all surrounding sponge creams.

Above: On Christmas Day 1805 plum puddings such as this were 'Rumbling in the pot' at Dove Cottage.

Below: Teatime cakes. Here are, from the back, thick and moulded gingerbreads, a rice cake, rice cake jumbles and cheesecakes.

mark 4 for 20 minutes, remove from the oven and allow to cool a little before transferring onto wire cooling racks.

On 6th November, 1800, Dorothy Wordsworth baked parkins.[34] The date is significant, for in the industrial West Riding, the centre of the north country parkin tradition, they had already become associated with Bonfire Night on November 5th ('Parkin Day' in Leeds), and was eaten over the next few days. [35] It would appear that Dorothy was following the practices of her mother's cousin, Miss Elizabeth Threlkeld of Halifax, with whom she spent her girlhood after her mother's death in 1778. Here, along with Miss Threlkeld's extended household of other orphaned nieces and nephews, parkins must have formed one of the most popular of all seasonal treats.

Parkins

7oz/200g medium oatmeal	*1tsp bicarbonate of soda*
7oz/200g flour	*8oz/225g black treacle*
1oz/25g brown sugar	*1oz/25g lard*
1½tsp ground ginger	*1oz/25g butter*

Thoroughly mix the oatmeal, flour, sugar, ginger and soda in a bowl, and make a well in the centre. Weigh the treacle into a saucepan, add the lard, butter, and 1tbs water, and stir over a gentle heat until just melted. Pour into the dry ingredients and stir until thoroughly mixed to form a soft dough.

Use a dessert spoon to form into balls about 2ins/5cm diameter, and place on a greased baking sheet leaving some 2ins/5cm between each one to allow them to spread. Bake at 150°C, 300°F, Gas mark 2 for 45 minutes, then remove onto a wire rack to cool. [36]

The American-style cheesecake, that heavy slab of creamy solidity mounted on a crushed-biscuit base found in every supermarket, has nothing in common with the English varieties, except for its name. In the north country cheesecakes came in the form of tartlets, their short pastry crusts being filled with the jam-like lemon curd or lemon cheese, with custardy rice mixtures, or, particularly in Yorkshire, with curds mixed with sugar, currants, nutmeg and eggs.

Lemon Cheesecakes

Lemon cheese, made to the recipe on page 142[37]

*Short pastry made with 8oz/225g flour, 2oz/50g butter and
2oz/50g lard, a pinch of salt, and about 3-4 tbs cold water.*

Use the pastry to line a dozen tart tins, fill with baking
beans, and bake at 200°C, 400°F, Gas mark 6 for 10-15
min., remove the beans, return to the oven for 5 min. and
allow to cool. Half fill the tarts with the lemon cheese, and
return to the oven at 180°C, 350°F, Gas mark 4 for 5-10
minutes, before removing and leaving to cool.

Joanna's recipe for a rice cheesecake is amongst the most unusual in
this collection, its combination of ingredients being unlike almost
any of those found in the most popular cookery books of the period.
The results, even if baked with skill, certainly fall into the category of
'interesting', rather than 'good'.

Rice Cheese Cakes

*Boil 4oz of rice, put it in a sieve to drain 4 Eggs well beaten, ½lb
Butter ½ pint of Cream, 6oz of Sugar nutmeg, a glass of Ratafia
or Brandy, beat well together, & bake them in paste.*[38]

1oz/25g pudding rice	⅛pt/75ml double cream
2oz/50g butter	1tbs brandy
1½oz/35g sugar	⅛tsp grated nutmeg
1 egg, beaten	
shortcrust pastry made from :	
8oz/225g flour, 4oz/100g butter (or lard, or ½ butter,	
½ lard), and 3-4 tbs cold water.	

Use the pastry to prepare a dozen blind-baked tarts as in
the previous recipe. Simmer the rice in ½pt/300ml water
for about 20 min. until tender, then drain. Cream the
butter and sugar, beat in the eggs little by little, and beat
in the cream, brandy and nutmeg. The butter in this recipe
will separate out unless the mixture is very well beaten
at every stage. Stir in the rice, ³/₄ fill the tarts and bake at

150°C, 300°F, Gas mark 2 for 20-25 min. until the tops are
a pale golden brown.

Throughout the Wordsworths' years at Grasmere and Rydal, most of
the working population of the Lake District still relied heavily on the
local, home-baked oatcake, as they had probably done for millennia.
Oats were still grown here, flourishing far better than wheat, and,
after being dried, were ground between gritstone stones in all the
smaller mills, the Wordsworths' supply almost certainly coming from
Tongue Gill Mill, on the Dunmail Raise side of Grasmere. At their
cottage, they appear to have used oats only to make their porridge, but
they certainly enjoyed the oatcakes offered to them by neighbours,
farmer's wives etc. When visiting the last farmhouse in Martindale,
for example, William was grateful for the 'welcome refreshment [to
which] the good woman treated us with oaten cake, new and crisp'.[39]
Dorothy was even more appreciative:

> 'And as for her, why Miss Wudsworth, she wad come into t'
> back kitchen an exe for a bit of oatcake and butter. She was
> fond of oatcake, and butter till it, fit to steal it a' most.'[40]

Compared to the Scottish oatcakes with which most people are now
familiar, that of the Lake District was of a distinctly superior quality. To
make it, the fresh-ground meal was first carefully sieved to extract the
finest oat-flour, the remainder being used for bannocks or porridge.
A small quantity was then mixed into a stiff dough with a little
warm water and clapped out on a wooden board until about twenty
inches/50cm in diameter and about one-sixteenth of an inch/2mm
in thickness. Since oats contain hardly any gluten, the ability to make
such cakes without them breaking up or cracking was a feat of real
skill, only acquired by being brought up to it from girlhood. Originally
they were baked by being slid onto a large flat slab of fireproof stone
supported a few inches above a peat fire on the hearth. The local source
of these was probably at the appropriately-named High Bakestones
between Scandale Fell and Dove Crag, three miles to the north-west of
Grasmere, as the crow flies. By the nineteenth century, however, many
had been replaced by large round plates of cast iron.[41] Although not of
the same size, oatcakes of the same thickness, crispness and flavour
can still be made today, using the following traditional recipe:-

Fig 14. The oatmeal for the oatcakes which Dorothy enjoyed at local farms, as well as for their breakfast porridge, was probably ground here at Tongue Ghyll Mill, just off the road from Grasmere towards Dunmail Raise. This drawing is by Sara Hutchinson, Wordsworth's niece.

Oatcake

4oz/100g fine oatmeal (Purchase 'fine oatmeal' from health food shops etc., pass it though a fine sieve to extract the fine 'flour', and retain the rest for making porridge etc.)

Place the sieved oat 'flour' into a small bowl and stir in a pinch of salt. Place a jug on the scales, weigh in 2oz/50g of tepid water, pour this into the oats, mix in and then knead rapidly to form a uniform dough. Scatter a thin layer of sieved oatmeal onto a board, place the ball of dough in the centre, and pat it out to form a 3ins/8cm disc, then press the centre down with the fingertips until about one sixteenth of an inch/2-3mm in thickness. Rotate it on its bed of dry oatmeal while extending the size to the thin central area, maintaining a thick even rim until it is about 8-9ins/20-22cm in diameter, then flatten the rim, and roll lightly to ensure an even thickness. By now it should be over 10ins/25cm in diameter. Place an upturned dinner plate on top, and cut off the uneven edges, to produce a perfect circle.

Place a circular iron girdle over a gentle heat until a sprinkling of flour browns very slowly, but does not smoke. Brush off the flour, very lightly grease the girdle, slide on the oatcake, using a piece of thick paper or thin card to transfer it from the board, and leave to cook until crisp, with slightly raised edges, but not browned. Finally remove from the girdle, and cool on a wire tray.

If no girdle is available, the oatcake may be slid onto a baking tray, and baked at 180°C, 350°F, Gas mark 4 for 15 min. Remove from the tray and leave to cool on a wire tray.

Chapter Seven

OF SWEETS

At the opening of the nineteenth century most large towns had a number of confectioners making fruit drops, comfits, tablets, candies, chocolates, lozenges, fruit pastes and mint cakes. Theirs was a highly-skilled profession, requiring specialist knowledge and equipment, but a number of the simpler sweets could be easily made in ordinary homes. Cumbrian youngsters used to enjoy 'Taffy-joinin's' for example, clubbing their pennies together to buy treacle etc. for a winter evening's toffee-making, at which the smearing of each other's faces provided great fun.[1]

Toffee

Take 4oz: of Butter, 4 of Sugar, and 4 of Treacle, half the rind of a large lemon grated and a quarter of a teaspoonful of pounded ginger mix them all together and boil them over a slow fire until the Toffee becomes crisp (which you must ascertain by dropping a little of it into cold water) then pour it into a Tin and cut it out when cold.[2]

4oz/100g butter	*grated zest of ½ lemon*
4oz/100g sugar	*¼tsp ground ginger*
4oz/100g black treacle	

Rub the base and sides of a shallow baking tin with a little butter, and set aside. Boil the remaining ingredients together, stirring constantly over a gentle heat, until a drop plunged into cold water rapidly forms a hard ball. Pour into the tin, allow to cool, then break up when completely set.

Alternatively the top may be marked out into squares when half-set using a buttered knife, so that it may be easily broken up into neat pieces when cold.

The Fricker family made two other sweets which may now be served at the end of a meal, or at parties. The first, called 'Strengthening Jelly' is an original form of wine-gum which slowly releases its rich flavour and alcohol as it dissolves in the mouth.

Strengthening Jelly

2oz of Isinglass, 2oz brown sugar, 1oz Gum arabic, 1 small nutmeg grated, the above to be boiled in a quart of Port or very good white wine, then strained when cold cut into small pieces the size of a nutmeg, & one occasionally put into the mouth.[3]

1tbs brown (Demarara) sugar	*4tsp gelatin*
½pt/300ml port or strong white wine	*¼ grated nutmeg*

Mix the ingredients in a pan, set aside for 5 minutes, then stir and heat until the gelatin and sugar have completely dissolved. Strain through a piece of muslin into jug, and leave until lukewarm, then pour into a metal or thin plastic box some 4-5ins/10-15cm square, and leave in a cool place until set firmly.

Dip the box briefly in warm water, and turn the jelly out on to a piece of wet muslin or greaseproof paper, and use a knife dipped in hot water to cut it into ½ins/1·5cm squares, arranging these separately on a serving dish or plate.

The second has a lemon or orange flavour, lightened by being whipped just before being left to set;

Sponge Cream

One ounce & ½ of Isinglass dissolved in a pint of water, the rind and juice of three large lemons, one orange, rather more than half a pound of loaf sugar, which rub upon the lemon and orange peel, mix all together and whisk it an hour when cold cut it in square pieces.[4]

9tsp gelatin	*8oz/225g lump sugar*
3 lemons	*1 orange*

Sprinkle then stir the gelatin into 1pt/600ml cold water, leave for 5 min., then stir in a pan over a gentle heat, or microwave for 1 min., until it has dissolved, then set aside. Rub the sugar lumps on the lemon and orange peels to extract their oils and colour, then squeeze their juice (which should produce ½pt/150ml), and strain it through a piece of muslin. Add both the sugar and the juice to the gelatin mixture, and stir (gently warming if necessary) until completely dissolved, then set aside until cold and just beginning to set.

Turn the jelly into a metal bowl set in a bowl of iced water and whisk until it has turned into a white foam. Pour into a deep metal tray or loaf tin in a ¾ins/2cm deep layer, leave in a cool place to set overnight, then turn out onto a sheet of wet muslin or greaseproof paper, and use a knife dipped into warm water to cut it into cubes. Arrange these on a dish, and serve.

Chapter Eight

OF PRESERVES & PICKLES

Today we can enjoy most foods throughout each year, but this has been achieved only through the development of freezing, canning and the rapid international transport of fresh foods. In the opening years of the nineteenth century there was still a great reliance on locally-grown seasonal foods, many of which were only available for a few weeks at a time. In order to enable them to be enjoyed beyond this period, the methods of home-preservation were quite limited, sugar being the main preservative for fruit, and salt and/ or vinegar for vegetables. Some attempts were made to keep fruits etc. without any of these additives, in order to retain their original flavours intact as can be seen in this recipe. Boiling in bottles sterilised them very effectively, but the use of corks and rosin to provide an airtight seal was not particularly reliable, and if they failed, the contents would quickly decay.

Green gooseberries to Bottle

gather gooseberries before full grown, pick and put them into clean bottle with as much cold water as the Bottles (when nearly full of gooseberries) will hold. set them without corks into a pan of cold water over the fire, let them remain 'till scalded take them out when cold, cork & Rosin the Bottles
NB. if the Bottles are full they will burst.[1]

However, the success-rate of this method was greatly increased when sugar was added to the fruit. Not only did this form an excellent preserving syrup, but it also provided the housewife or housekeeper with a new convenience food.

Dorothy Wordsworth used sugar when preserving her gooseberries in August 1800, but, although in her late 20s, was still uncertain as to the best proportions of sugar to fruit. She therefore decided to experiment, noting in her journal 'Boiled gooseberries N.B. 2lbs of sugar in the first panful, 3 quarts all good measure 3lbs in the 2nd 4 quarts 2¹/₂lbs in the third.'[2] Assuming that all were bottled and sealed while still scalding hot, she should have had good results with each batch, only varying in their relative sweetness. Now she could open a bottle or jar whenever required to provide a dish of sweet, cooked fruit ready to be eaten with cream, to garnish a dessert, to fill pies, or to go into puddings. Other fruits could be preserved in the same way: These are Joanna's recipes.

Green Gage Plumbs

Put the plumbs (not quite ripe) into a Pan of Spring Water with the vine leaves, set them on a slow fire, when the skins begin to rise take them off & skin them carefully, put them on a sieve as you do them, then put them into the same water, cover them close & hang them at a great distance from the fire till they are green, which will be 5 or 6 hours at least. drain them. make a good syrup & give them a gentle boil in it twice a day for 4 days [before bottling][3]

Green Apricots to preserve

Gather the Apricots before the stones are hard, put them in a Pan of spring water with vine leaves, set them over a slow fire till yellow, take them out, rub them with a flannel & salt to take off the peal, put them into the same water & leaves cover them close, set them by the fire till they are yellow, then take them carefully out, and boil them two or three times in a thin syrup, when they look plump & clear make a thicker syrup of fine sugar. & give the apricots a quick boil in it.
N.B. for Tarts boil them in the first syrup.[4]

To preserve fruit of any kind

Gather the fruit when dry & to a pint of fruit take ¼lb Lump sugar (or fine soft will do), put the fruit & sugar into jars or wide necked Bottles a layer of sugar and a layer of fruit.
Tye the jars down with wet bladders, set them in a pan of cold water on the fire. let it boil full half an hour, or until you think the fruit is enough done. Take it off the fire and let the jars stand in it until it is stone cold, then cover the bladders with double paper. Apples, Pears, Siberian Crabs, may be done in this way.[5]

Mary Wordsworth used this method to preserve their damsons, this popular local fruit thus being converted from a sour plum into one of the most succulent luscious and richly flavoured of all preserves. It is well worth the effort of making today, either to serve cold with cream or ice-cream, hot with custard, or baked either in a pie or under a crumble.

[To Preserve Damsons]

To one pt of Damsons put 6oz of Sugar, tie the bottles over with bladders & bake after the bread is drawn [6]

Damsons Sugar

Fill a number of screw-topped jam jars with damsons, and shake in enough sugar to cover them (this gives the same proportions of fruit to sugar as the original recipe). Place, without lids, on baking trays, and bake at 150°C, 300°F, Gas mark 2 for some 30 min. by which time all the sugar should have dissolved to form a rich maroon syrup, and the damsons have split their skins. Remove from the oven, allow to cool a little, then screw on their sterilised lids.

The Wordsworths also made their own Seville Orange marmalade from fruit imported from Spain and Portugal. The earlier form of English marmalade had been a thick paste made from whole oranges, sometimes boiled with pippins, but the potted jam type, with strips of the peel added to give a more interesting texture and flavour, had already been adopted here by the 1670s. [7]

Marmalade

An equal weight of the cleanest Seville oranges & loaf Sugar Take off the rinds, boil them until Tender Scrape all the pulp from skin and seed. When the rinds are sufficiently boild 1½ hours cut them as thin as possible wiping the knife often else it will make them black. Put rind, pulp & juice in a preserving pan with the sugar boil over a slow fire about 40 or 50 minutes put it jars [cover?] when cold with brandy papers & tie them down close [8]

Seville oranges, and their weight of sugar.

Remove the peels from the oranges, and simmer these in plenty of water for about an hour until tender. Drain, allow to cool, and use a spoon to scrape off most of the pith, and cut the rind into narrow shreds. Slice the oranges thinly, removing the seeds and surplus pith, put into a pan with the shredded peel, sugar, and enough water to cover them, and stew gently for 40-50min. until they have come to a dark, jam-like consistency. If too thick, a little water may be added as they cook. Pour into sterilised jars and seal down.

Lemon curd, or lemon cheese, was probably the most popular lemon preserve. Both lemons and sugar were imported directly into the Fricker sisters' home town of Bristol:

Lemon Cheese

Grate the rind of 3 Lemons, then add the juice, & mix with it 8 ounces of Loaf sugar, 4?ounces of butter the yolks of 6 and the whites of 4 eggs well beaten set it over the fire in a saucepan, – keep stirring it until quite dissolved, and it begins to thicken take great care not to let it brown.

Then pour it into jars for use cover it like preserves with paper dipped in brandy, when you make Cheesecakes lay paste in your pattypans and half fill them with the mixture.
N.B. this mixture will keep a long time in jars well covered, in a cool place. [9]

3 small or 2 large lemons	3oz/75g butter
8oz/225g sugar	4 yolks & 3 whites of egg

Grate the zest from the lemons, put it into a saucepan with their strained juice, the sugar, butter and beaten and strained eggs. Stir continuously over a gentle heat until the mixture has thickened, then pour into sterilised jars, seal down, and keep for use, either for making lemon cheesecakes (*see p.126*), as a spread, or as a sauce on hot puddings, cold cheesecakes or ice-cream.

Jelly made from red or white currants was useful either as a preserve, or as an accompaniment to both hot and cold cooked meats. Joanna Hutchinson's recipe cooks the currants with sugar before passing them through a flannel filter bag,but this is a very slow process, particularly when it is cold. For this reason the modernised version below only adds the sugar after the juice has already been extracted and filtered.

Red or white Currant Jelly

Pick the currants very clean, to 1lb of fruit, 1lb of loaf sugar pounded, mix it in a pan, set them on a slow fire, stirring all the time, let it boil 5 minutes, then pass it thro' a flannel Bag into Glasses.[10]

1lb/450g red or white currants   *1lb/450g sugar*

Stew the currants with ⅓pt/200ml water for about 30 min. stirring from time to time to prevent them from sticking, then pour into a jelly bag or cloth hung over a clean pan and leave for about 12 hours. Add the sugar to the juice, heat gently while stirring, until it has dissolved, then boil rapidly for about 15 min., skimming it carefully. Test a little on a cold saucer, until it reaches setting point, then pour into sterilised jars and seal down.

Some imported preserves, such as ginger in syrup, were quite expensive. This led would-be fashionable housewives and housekeepers to make their own by flavouring lettuce stalks with ground ginger and sugar. The following version from Mary Wordsworth's recipe book is quite typical:

Artificial Ginger

When the Cos Lettuces are running to seed cut off the leaves & peel the stalks till quite clear cut them in pieces & throw them into water as you do them wash well – & have ready a syrup of sugar & water 5 pints to a lb & with some powdered Ginger tied up in a bag boil for 20 minutes set it aside for 2 days boil again for ½ an hour repeat the boiling 5 or 6 times leaving a day or two between then drain it & wipe the pieces quite dry make a syrup (a lb to a pint of water) of sugar & [mix] with a good deal of ginger well scraped & sliced boil it in them 2 or 3 times till quite clear & taste like Indian Ginger. at the last boiling put in the peel & juice of one Lemon.[11]

There were three distinct varieties of vinegar available from Georgian grocers and oilmen, the true vinegars made from either red or white wine, and the alegar made from malted liquors, which we know today as malt vinegar. All were useful preservatives and condiments, the wine vinegars giving more gentle and refined flavours than the much more robust alegars. However, since many households took pride in their self-sufficiency, and wished to avoid the probably dangerously adulterated purchased supplies, it was quite usual for families such as the Hutchinsons and Frickers to make their own:

Vinegar (Mrs Charlton's)

1¼lbs of coarse brown Sugar to every Gal. of Water, boil & skin it, pour it into a Tub to cool, when milk warm put it into the Cask with a little Yeast, set it in the Sun. Cover the Bung hole with a brown paper full of holes.[12]

Sugar Vinegar

one pound and a half of sugar, to one gallon of water boil it half an hour put it into a Tub to ferment with a little Barm upon a Toast for two days, put it into a Barrel, bung it up (not too close). Let it stand in a warm place until sour then bottle it.[13]

Pickles must have played a useful role in planning meals at Dove Cottage, enlivening the previously roasted and boiled joints when they reappeared cold over the next day or two, in addition to providing a fashionable accompaniment to the more formal dinners prepared for visiting friends. Compared to most of today's pickles, those of late Georgian England were very highly spiced, using the same ingredients and similar recipes to those that East India Company employees had first experienced during their sojourns on the sub-continent. The yellow pickle made by the Hutchinson sisters is typical in the use of salt to remove the surplus moisture from its vegetables and the use of a heavily-spiced alegar as a combined flavouring and preservative. The appearance of long pepper is a little unexpected, for it had gone out of general use in English cookery in the early seventeenth century, and never regained its former popularity. Sharper, hotter and sweeter than black pepper and in catkin-like spikes of tiny seeds about 2½ins/6cm long, it came from two separate species of shrub, one from the Himalayan foothills and southern India, and the other from

Java and Malaysia. In the late eighteenth century it became available again through the East India trade, but today can be very difficult to find. For this reason, it has been replaced by black pepper in the modernised recipe below.

Yellow Pickle

Take Cabbage, Carrots, Turnips, Cauliflowers, Apples, or any thing else you like, cut them into pieces, put them in a pan of boiling water for a minute, then drain them put them into a close pot with a good quantity of salt, press them down with a Weight let them remain for three days then dry them in the sun or by the fire 2 q.ts of Alegar, 2oz. Ginger, 2oz. White Mustard seed, 1oz. Long Pepper, 2oz garlic, 1oz White Pepper & plenty of Cayenne and a little Turmeric (steeped in vinegar & strained) to colour the vegetables The Pickle need not be boiled [14]

> *1lb/450g each of cabbage, carrot, turnip, cauliflower,*
> *and apple, cut in pieces around ½ ¾ins/1·5 2cm cubes*
>
> | | |
> |---|---|
> | *2tsp white peppercorns* | *1pt/600ml malt vinegar* |
> | *½oz/12g root ginger, sliced* | *6oz/150g salt* |
> | *1tsp turmeric* | *2tsp black pepper* |
> | *4tsp white mustard seed* | *½tsp cayenne pepper* |
> | *4 cloves of garlic, sliced* | |

Bring a large pan of water to the boil, put in a batch of vegetables for a minute, then use a sieve or a pierced spoon to remove them into a bowl. Boil further batches in the same way, then leave the vegetables until quite cold. Layer the vegetables and the salt in a cylindrical saucepan, put a plate on top, then a weight, and leave in a cool place for the next 3 days.

Meanwhile divide the vinegar between two jars, stirring the turmeric into one, and the remaining spices in the other, cover, and leave to soak. Finally, drain the vegetables, pat them dry using a towel, and pack into jars. Pass the turmeric vinegar through a coffee filter paper, mix with the spiced vinegar, and use to fill up the jars before sealing them down. This crisp, hot and spicy pickle may be used after a couple of weeks.

In common with most recipes for pickled mushrooms, this version from Joanna Hutchinson's notebook imbues their usual mild flavour with one much more pungent and spicy. If a more subtle pickle is preferred, replace the 'alegar' with white wine vinegar.

Pickled Mushrooms (brown)

Rub the Mushrooms with a flannel & Alegar; 2qts. of good Strong Alegar, 4 spoonfuls of salt, ¼oz. Mace, ½oz Nutmegs, 2 drams Cayenne Pepper, ¼lb Anchovies, washed & picked, a large Lemon Peel, ½oz. Cloves put in the Mushrooms when the pickle boils, & let them simmer 20 minutes.[15]

Contents of a 50g tin of anchovies, drained	
1½lb/675g button mushrooms	*1tsp salt*
½ a nutmeg, finely chopped & rinsed	*½tsp mace*
1pt/600ml malt vinegar	*10 cloves*
pared zest of ½ lemon	*⅛tsp cayenne pepper*

Use a cloth or sponge dipped in vinegar to rub all smuts etc. from the mushrooms, rubbing from the top downwards to avoid tearing the skin and gills. Bring the remaining ingredients to the boil, add the mushrooms, and simmer for 20 min. Pack the mushrooms into jars, cover with the liquid, and seal down. They may be used either immediately, or over the following year.

The lemon pickle used to accompany curries in India was often replicated in English middle-class kitchens, using imported lemons and spices. Early eighteenth century recipes are for relatively simple methods, such as boiling in salted water and potting in white wine vinegar.[16] By 1800 the lemons were being salted, dried, spiced and pickled in processes taking around three months, after which some cooks discarded the lemons, retaining their liquor for flavouring white or brown sauces: 'It is a most useful pickle, and give a fine flavour to whatever it is to be used in. But remember always to put it in before you thicken the sauce, or put in any cream, lest the sharpness should make it curdle, which will spoil your sauce.'[17] In the modernised version below, the lemons are slowly dried in the oven rather than by sunlight, the latter commodity always being unpredictable in England, and even more so in the Lake District. Oven drying was also recommended by

John Farley, cook to the famous London Tavern, in his popular book *The London Art of Cookery*, first published in 1783.[18]

To pickle Lemons

Take 12 Lemons cut them across into 4 parts downwards but not quite thro', then put in as much salt as they will hold, rub them well & strew them over with it, let them lie in an Earthen Dish in the Sun & turn them every day, cut an oz. of Ginger very thin & 12 cloves of garlic salted for 3 days a small handful of Mustard Seed bruised one Pod of Red Indies Pepper to every Lemon, take the Lemons when dry, put them into a jar with juice & other ingredients, & cover with best white wine Vinegar They will be ready for use in 4 months, add Vinegar as the Pickle is used.[19]

½pt/300ml white wine vinegar	6 lemons
6oz/150g large crystal sea salt	6 dried red chillies or
½oz/12g root ginger, sliced thin	1tsp cayenne pepper
6 cloves of garlic, peeled	2tbs mustard seed

Take each lemon in turn, hold it upright with the stalk end uppermost, and make two diametric cuts almost down to the pointed top, to divide it into four equal segments. Ease the joints open, pack them with the salt, place in a baking dish, and leave to rest overnight.

Next day bake at 110°C, 225°F, Gas mark ¼ for 2 hours, and leave until perfectly cold. Very gently squeeze most of the juice (not the pulp) from each lemon, then strain all the liquid through a muslin-lined sieve to remove the surplus salt. Pack the lemons into one or two jars, pour in the strained juice, add the garlic, spices and bruised mustard seed, top up with the vinegar, seal down, and keep in a cool place for 4 months before using.

This lemon pickle has a remarkable saline/sour taste much more characteristic of oriental than English cuisine. In contrast, the practice of pickling unripe walnuts, as carried on here from the early eighteenth century, produces a rather fuller, spicier flavour.[20]

Walnuts to Pickle

Prick the Walnuts with a pin, put them in soft water, change it every day for a month, then put them in strong salt & water for a fortnight then take them out & wipe them clean Take vinegar Ginger, black pepper (Garlic) & any other warm seasoning boil them all with the vinegar & pour it upon the Walnuts, heat it 3 or 4 times & put it upon the Walnuts before they are closed up.[21]

Walnuts, salt, malt vinegar, root ginger, black pepper, garlic

The young green walnuts must be picked before the end of June, after which their shells become too hard for pickling. Wearing rubber gloves to prevent the hands being stained, prick each walnut all over with a long, strong needle. The preliminary 1 month soaking may be replaced by brining twice, soaking them in a brine of 3oz/75g salt to each pint/·5l of water for one week, then putting them in a fresh batch of the same strength of brine for a second week, then drain and wipe dry.

Make spiced vinegar by boiling ½oz/12g bruised root ginger, ½tsp black pepper and 3 cloves of garlic, chopped, to each pint of vinegar for 10 minutes, then leaving it to cool. Pack the walnuts into jars, cover with the strained vinegar, seal down and leave for 6 to 8 weeks before using.

Chapter Nine

OF CHEESE & CURDS

Dairying in most Lakeland farms was carried out almost as much to serve the statesmen and their families as it was to produce a cash income. Much of the milking took place in the fields,some Cumbrian farms growing 'milkin' rings' of overhanging trees or bushes, usually holly, to provide a sheltered area for milking their cows in hot weather, one being noted at Causeway Foot near Keswick.[1] Having been carried back to the farm in wooden piggins or pails, the milk was strained through a muslin-based 'sile' into broad pans, and left overnight to allow the cream to rise to the surface. This was then removed by being blown off into a cream-kit.[2] Most of the cream was preserved by being converted into butter, cream-cheeses or cream curds, and much of the remaining blown- or blue-milk into either 'whangy cheese', or 'cum't milk', a dish made by curdling it with rennet.[3] The best farmhouse cheeses were made of whole milk curdled with rennets made from either the cured fourth stomach of a calf called a keslop skin, or the juice of Lady's Bedstraw, Galium verum, locally known as 'cheese-rennet'.[4] The curds were then placed in a muslin-lined cylindrical open-topped tub called a cheese-ring, and pressed to remove the remaining whey. Weighing some 10 to 12lbs each, these cheeses were then either stored for home use, or sold at the nearest markets.[5] It would have been cheese of this kind that the Wordsworths would have enjoyed with home-made bread when calling at John Stanley's at the King's Head, Thirlspot.[6]

Since there was neither space nor time to keep even a house-cow at Dove Cottage, all the milk and cream they required had to be bought in. In February 1802 Jenny Dockray brought a present of milk from her farmhouse at either Underhow or Butterlip How on the Easedale road. This appears to have been their main source of dairy produce, for in November 1801 Dorothy recorded how: 'We walked into Easedale to gather mosses and fetch cream. I went for the cream and sat under a wall. It was piercing cold and a hail storm came in the afternoon.'[7] On 30th April, 1802 a much more regular supply was obtained when Dorothy 'Began to get Milk from F. Baty's 1d in the Evening', Frank Baty, or Bateman, living nearby at Town End.[8] In the spring of 1804, when Molly Fisher took over the running of her brother's house on the opposite side of the road to Dove Cottage, she also looked after his single cow. This probably provided a more convenient source, including cream for Johnny Wordsworth's porridge and presents of pounds of butter.[9] A couple of years later William's one surviving daughter Dora would see the theme of her nursery rhyme 'Cushy cow bonny, let down thy milk' enacted here by Old Molly.[10] Shortly after the Wordsworths moved into Allan Bank in 1808 the newly-available land and staff made it possible for them to acquire a house-cow, Dorothy telling Clarkson in December that 'We keep a cow the stable is two short field lengths from the house, and the cook has both to fodder and clean after the cow.'[11] This provided all the household's milk and cream, the latter being churned to supply butter too.[12]

The introduction of dairying into the Wordsworth household was undoubtedly due to the previous experience of the Hutchinson sisters, who had kept house-cows for many years at Sockburn, and Gallow Hill. Their depth of knowledge is admirably demonstrated by the following advice which Sara sent to Mary Monkhouse who was apparently setting up a dairy at Tom Hutchinson's farm at Hindwell, Radnorshire:

> & as the for Churn I can do nothing for you the one Mr. Taylor recommended was Beetham's (patent Churn I believe) he lives in London But I dare say there are by this time improvements upon it Mr Taylor's only churn 12lb and a churn of that shape to churn only a firkin [56lb] would be very awkward I saw one advertised in the Courier yesterday; but it was a patent one also - & only made in Lancashire J. Woods, Ormskirk - It is worked by a lever with a weight & grit & performs more work with it than 2 women in the same time without it & price £2.12.6. What kind of Churns are used in the County? I would on no account advise you to get one that does not work with a Churn staff next to this a barrel churn is best that turns round altogether but then it requires most art in churning - & some people always churn ill with them (our Betty for instance).[13]

Getting a good dairymaid, ideally one with cold hands that did not spoil the butter, was to remain a problem. As Mary explained to Sara, then at Grassy Nook near Stockton on Tees,

'I dropped the thought of a servant from you as soon as I had sent my [last] letter off, for it occurred to me that a Durham or Yorkshire lass would not do in our cowhouse we have not got one nor heard of any.'[14]

By 1811, now transferred to Grasmere Rectory, the dairying activities were expanded by buying more cows to serve the needs of the family, as well as producing a surplus for sale. In early May, 1812, after a winter on hay, and before the benefits of new grass began to show, Dorothy noted that 'The cows do not give so much milk as they did, but very well considering we expect to sell butter this week. It is 14d pr. lb. As we have plenty of hay it is very well we kept the great cow & We have already got a guinea's worth of butter from her besides the calf a guinea and about 4/- new milk at Mr. Crump's, besides all the blue milk which we have sold, and we have not yet got a pig.'[15] The butter was made up for sale using carved wooden moulds called prints. While staying at Hindwell in October 1814, Dorothy received a note from young Dora, reminding her that 'Mary Dawson said I was to tell you not to forget the butter prints' which were to be used for this purpose.[16]

If butter was to be preserved either for sale or for use over winter, it had a little more salt than usual beaten into it and was packed down into airtight containers, barrels for large quantities, and ceramic jars for small, especially on a domestic scale. Martha Fricker used the following brining technique:

To Pot Butter

1 Teaspoonful of Salt Petre, to two Teaspoonfuls of white & finely beaten sugar & three spoonfuls of salt. To be pounded & boiled up with a little water, & when cold, poured on the Jar of butter, & covering close to the top of the Jar.[17]

The making of large hard cheeses was impractical in such a small household, but more delicate soft cheeses provided a pleasant addition to the Wordsworths' regular diet. The following recipe comes from Mary's recipe book:

[A Soft Cheese]

The Vat must be a plated Seive The Cheese Cloth thin muslin. To 3 qts of new milk & one of thick cream a little warm put as much Rennet as will make it come pretty stiff then put it into the Cheese vat lined with the muslin. lay on it a light sinker & weight till it comes to 4 pd. the next day turn it out on boards & salt & ....Cover it with nettles and if the weather is hot it will ripe in a week.[18]

Very similar home-made soft cheeses were made by her sister Joanna:

[Cheese]

Take 2 qts of Cream & 2 qts of New Milk warm from the Cow, if not warm enough to cum pour in a little boiling Water, a Table spoonful of [rennet] is sufficient, when it is turned take it into a fine Cloth & squeeze it, but not break the Curd if wanted to eat soon you must mould it in oval or round dish about 1½inches deep, turn it every day with a fresh Cloth wet & well wrung, let it be upon the Table so that the Whey may drain from it, and press it with a weight, then put it between 2 Pewter plates to ripen & it will be fit to eat in 4 days, if wanted sooner put Nettles round it & send it to Table upon Currant Leaves.[19]

Today virtually all available milk and cream has already been pasteurised. Cheese rennet, meanwhile, is almost unobtainable, while alternative curdling agents such as lemon juice or vinegar impart unwelcome flavours. For these reasons the above recipes are not really practical in a modern kitchen, but this Hutchinson version still gives good results, a delicious home-made cream cheese:

Cream Cheese

Take a qt of thick Cream out of the cream Pot, stir a little salt in it, & lay it upon a fine Cloth, & put it into a Hair Sieve (the Cloth must be wet) turn it once or twice a day till stiff & send it to Table.[20]

1pt/600ml double cream   *2tsp salt*

Rinse a 12ins/30cm square of fine muslin, wring it out, and use to line a sieve with as few creases as possible, then place the sieve over a bowl. Double cream can vary considerably in its consistency, so add the salt and whisk until a small cone remains on the surface on removing the whisk, otherwise the cream will probably run straight through the muslin. Leave overnight, in a cool place, then invert onto another square of freshly-rinsed muslin, and replace in the sieve for a further 12 hours. By this time it will be reasonably stiff and have a delicate flavour, which improves if kept for 3 or 4 days, turning it once or twice each day.

Cream curds were a popular dessert in many households where there was access to cream, milk, eggs and buttermilk. To make them, a very lightly egged mix of milk and eggs was poured into a very large pan of salted water with just sufficient buttermilk to form a soft curd, which was then drained on a muslin-lined sieve. When cold and completely drained, the curds were turned out onto a dish and served with redcurrant jelly and a sprinkling of sugar. However, in common with other apparently straightforward recipes, the production of good curds depended more on long experience of dairy practice than on the ability to follow a written recipe.

Cream Curds

Set on the Fire a brass Pan full of water with a little Salt, then take yolks of 4 Eggs well beaten & mix them with a pint of Cream & a pint of Milk; which when the water boils pour into the Pan with a small Tea Cup full of Butter-milk, When the Curd rises take it carefully out with a slice into a Muslin Bag spread upon a Seive.[21]

In the more prosperous later years at Rydal Mount the Wordsworths enjoyed Stilton cheese, which was supplied to them from London via Mr Powell, the poet and dramatist. As soon as the last one was about to be finished, Mary would ask him to arrange for others to be despatched northwards, where their arrival was eagerly anticipated. Those that their servant Ann unpacked in August 1837 were a great disappointment: 'one having been nibbled by Rats [was] brought in at dinner. To my dismay it is no Stilton what they may call the kind I know not, but it is not nearly so good or so rich as our Lancashire; of a hard stiff texture, and two weighing 13½ [lb] each. As Mr P. had no doubt ordered Stiltons it would be proper that he should know his orders were disobeyed. He is not the cheesemonger whose card was enclosed in the Packet.' [22] With her personal knowledge of dairy produce, Mary was not to be fobbed off with substandard cheeses, and no doubt eventually obtained full satisfaction from the suppliers.

Chapter Ten

OF DRINKS

'To drink wild water, and to pluck green herbs,' as William explained in *The Prelude*, engendered 'Pure passions, virtue, knowledge, and delight/The holy life of music and of verse'.[1] Pure, moving water was both symbolic of the plain living and high principles of the Romantic poets, and also a readily-available amenity at Dove Cottage. Described by Dorothy as 'the Syke as we call it, that diminutive Beck where we get our water', provided an unfailing supply.[2] In addition, there was a small round well which had to be cleaned out either by William or by John Fisher to keep it free from mud.[3] Eleanor Rawnsley considered that the Wordsworths were fortunate to have such a well in the garden, since tea was too expensive for them. In this she perpetuates a common myth of creative poverty, for they could always afford this most expensive beverage. It was certainly considered a real extravagance by many in Grasmere in 1802, as Betty Towers told Dorothy that the family of old Jim Jackson 'might have looked up with the best [here] if they had been careful ... The wife would make tea 4 or 5 times a day and sec folks for sugar! Then she would have nae Teapot but she would take the water out of a Brass pan on the fire and pour it on to the Tea in a quart pot. This all for herself, for she boiled the tea leaves always for her husband and their son.'[4]

In 1803 Dorothy was expecting the arrival of a box of tea from her brother-in-law, Captain John Wordsworth, commander of the East Indiaman The Earl of Abergavenny.[5] She later explained to Thomas de Quincey that 'the tea sold here being very bad and very dear, we always get ours from London.' They obtained their supplies from Mr. Twining, who had called at the cottage on 23rd August, 1800. It was Richard Twining, as Chairman of the Tea Dealers' Association, who had persuaded Prime Minister William Pitt in 1784 to remove the 100% import duty on tea, and replace it with a 12½% lump sum paid by the merchants. This virtually eliminated smuggling, and greatly encouraged the trade, reducing retail prices. The Wordsworths' practice was to order their tea, take delivery of it, and then ask their London brother Richard to settle their account for them perhaps ten months later, just before placing their next order.[6] In 1808-9 they owed £13. 4s,

Fig 16. The Wordsworths always bought their tea from Twinings, the leading tea merchants of the day.

but by January 1810 they had spent a further £31.16s for Twining's tea, although some of this represented a joint purchase with Mr Cookson of Kendal.[7] No wonder that they considered giving up tea-drinking at this point, but they still carried on, even after receiving a bill for a massive £45.10s in May 1810, this being for all the tea supplied by Twinings since 1808, Richard never having settled the earlier accounts.[8] Soon another order was put in, a whole chest of black tea being expected in November.[9] Similar orders were placed in later years, the varieties in 1813 being Souchong, Pekoe and another fine black tea.[10]

At Dove Cottage tea appears to have been taken in the parlour on most afternoons, but this location was often changed to suit particular circumstances. Sometimes it could be around the kitchen fire, at others in the orchard, while in June 1800 John and Dorothy carried a jug of tea to William who was fishing for pike at Rydal. He drank it on the roadside turf before returning home.[11] Tea was also found to be one of the best drinks for long walks on cold days, John Stanley, landlord of the King's Head at Thirlspot, providing it for the Wordsworths on one of their descents from Helvellyn as well as on their pedestrian journeys between Keswick and Grasmere.[12] Frequent invitations to take tea were also exchanged with many of their neighbours, including the Simpsons of High Broadrain and the Oliffs at the Hollins on the Keswick road, the Batys, Lloyds and Fishers in Grasmere, the Cockyns in Keswick, and the Ibbotsons of Ambleside.[13] It is not known how the tea was served by these families, but they probably followed the local tradition of providing a choice of either sugar and cream or a glass of rum to stir into each cupful.[14]

Coffee was also drunk at Dove Cottage, but probably not to the same extent as tea. It was about double the price of tea, and taken either at breakfast or after dinner, rather than being a general social drink. In November 1802 Dorothy appears to have used coffee as a mild stimulant after spending an afternoon in bed. Unfortunately she spilled some on her foot, causing a severe scald, which Mary treated with an application of vinegar. Even so, she was unable to get to sleep until 4am and had to spend the next day in bed.[15]

The usual way to make coffee was to use a finely perforated filter called a percolator, placing the ground beans in the bottom, pouring on hot water, and leaving it to drip through into the coffee pot below. The success of this method depended on having a percolator, and on the fineness of its filter. Coleridge's recipe relied on neither of these, using egg white to remove even the smallest particles to produce a good, strong clear beverage:

[To make Coffee, 1802]

One half of the white of an egg – a cup of tepid water after the egg has been beaten up – Water enough to make the Coffee moist whatever it be /– Then put in the ground Coffee (1 heaped Coffee cup to six cups of boiling water to be [added] after put in) mix up the Coffee with the beat up egg & tepid water/ then put it into the Coffee Boiler, & add boiling water in the proportion of 6 to 1 – put it on a quick fire – & let it boil up two or three times. Then throw it into the China or Silver Coffee pot thro' a strainer / After boil & decant the Coffee grains & use the Decantia instead of hot water next time [16]

    ½ raw egg white   6 level tbs ground coffee

Put ¼pt/150ml tepid water into a saucepan, beat in the egg white, and then the coffee. Pour in 1pt/600ml boiling water (he used water boiled with the dregs of his last batch of coffee), boil until it has risen twice, then pour through a fine strainer into the coffee pot.

On hot days something much cooler and refreshing was required. Cold water was always available, but this could be rendered more flavoursome by being used to make Imperial water, a mild lemonade. This is Joanna Hutchinson's recipe:

Imperial Water

¼lb cream of Tartar, 10oz of Sugar, 9 qts of water boiled 10 minutes, strain it into an earthen Pot upon the Rind of 3 Lemons [17]

    6pts/3·6l water   3½oz/90g sugar
    1oz/25g cream of tartar   pared zest of a lemon

Boil the water, cream of tartar and sugar for 10 minutes, pour onto the lemon zest in a large heatproof container, cover, allow to go cold, then seal in sterilised bottles and keep in a cool place ready for use.

Mary Wordsworth's recipe for ginger beer makes an excellent summertime drink, easily and quickly made, lasting for a few weeks, and containing no alcohol to blur the senses. It is quite sweet, with a flavour mid-way between the sharpness of lemons and the dry heat of ginger.

Ginger Beer

4 lb loaf Sugar pounded
3 Lemons Pared & cut in slices
3 oz Cream of Tartar
3 oz Ginger bruised tied in thin muslin
3 Galls of boiling water poured over it in a covered Vessel. stir it
well, let it stand all night, strain & bottle it.[18]

For 8 pints/4·8l take;   *1 lemon*
1lb 4oz/550g sugar   *1oz/25g cream of tartar*
1oz/25g ground ginger loosely tied in a 6ins/15cm square of
muslin

Pare the zest off the lemon, thinly slice the rest, and place in the bottom of a large heatproof container with the sugar, cream of tartar and ginger.

Bring 8pts/4·8l water to the boil separately, pour onto the lemon etc., cover with a lid and thick cloth and leave overnight, then carefully ladle out into clean bottles, without disturbing the sediment. The remaining liquid may then be poured into a jug, the sediment allowed to settle and the clear poured off into the last bottle. Cork or screw down, and store in a cool place for use.

The ginger beers made in some of the households visited by the Wordsworths were solutions of ginger, lemon and sugar fermented with yeast. In addition to being alcoholic, these versions were effervescent and could cause problems if high pressure built up within their containers. Years later, at Rydal Mount, a gift of 'a most capital Beverage' from John Monkhouse had just been bottled by their servants, Willy and James, and the corks tied down, when two bottles exploded. This was probably due to their yeast being re-activated by 'the warm hands, or the warm air of the household [which] did the mischief'. The strings were immediately cut and the corks raised to prevent any further accidents, only being replaced a day or two later in the safety and coolness of the cellar.[19] A bung blown out of a cask might lead to the loss of it contents, but a bottle sealed too tightly could explode like a grenade without any warning whatsoever, sending particles of glass flying in all directions. For this reason it is best either to cork the bottles lightly or to use plastic drinks bottles when trying the recipes today.

Ginger Beer

Boil 4 quarts of water 4lbs of loaf sugar 1oz of pounded ginger for 20 minutes – Pare the rind of 4 lemons & squeeze the juice into a Cask – when the liquor is cool put it into the Cask with 1 table spoonful of yeast. let it remain in this state 4 days, then bottle it for use.[20]

8pts/4·8l water	*4 lemons*
4lbs/1·8kg sugar	*1 tbs dried yeast*
3 tbs ground ginger	

Boil the water, sugar and ginger in a large pan for 5 min., add the pared zest and strained juice of the lemons, and leave to cool to 36°C, 95°F. Take out a cupful of the liquid, beat the yeast into it until completely dissolved, then return it to the pan, and stir thoroughly. Cover the pan and leave at room temperature for 4 days, wrapping in a cloth or towel to prevent it chilling, if necessary.

At the end of this period fermentation should have largely ceased, so transfer the clear liquid into bottles, lightly corking them if glass, or screwing down if plastic, leave in the warm for a further day, then keep cool ready for use.

The recipe used by Joanna was virtually identical, except that it used a quarter of the proportion of sugar, and added egg whites and shells to clarify the initial solution:

Mrs Hugessons Ginger Beer

Boil 6 galls of water, 6lb soft sugar, 6oz Ginger beat fine, let it boil on hour, clarifying it with the Whites & shells of 6 Eggs beat well together, scum it, run it through a bag into an open vessel, let it stand to cool, then add the Juice & Rinds of 6 Lemons with two spoonfuls of yeast, put it into a cask, let it stand a fortnight more & it will be ready for use.[21]

Ale and beer were the general drinks throughout most homes in the Lake District. Those who drank very little, or lacked the necessary equipment, would buy in what they needed from a local inn or ale-house. Here, of course, supplies were constantly available for all customers, such as the Wordsworths, who snacked on bread and ale at the King's Head, Thirlspot, on their journeys between Grasmere and Keswick.[22] As early as February 1801 William was able to offer visitors to Dove Cottage his own 'little beer'. This was probably home-brewed, Dorothy finding that her 'brother had indeed been in much better health since we began to drink the ordinary ale which we brew ... We are now drinking the last cask of our own ale' in May, 1804.[23] This interval in home brewing did not mark a return to drinking water, but the arrival of a cask of strong brown stout, a present from Sir George and Lady Beaumont. Thinking of them, wrote Dorothy in her letter of thanks, ' will add not a little to the good effects of this liquor; we shall all drink of it, though we were educated and lived by choice as water-drinkers for many years after we grew up we have, for different reasons, all been obliged to drink malt liquor ... We shall, as you were so good as to direct, put a tea cup full of sweet Oil into the Cask'.[24] The olive oil formed an airtight seal across the upper surface of the stout, ensuring that it did not turn sour as slowly drawn off over the following months. In a letter to Lady Beaumont at the end of July, Dorothy told her of the 'pleasure I have received from drinking of the Brown Stout, of which I take a certain quantity every day and it seems to make me stronger and do me good.'[25]

There is no evidence to suggest the strength of the Wordsworths' home-brewed ale, but it was probably similar to that of the Fricker family, which, using only 1·8 bushels of malt to each barrel, was a small beer, just over half the strength of common country ale. It was a good everyday drink, however:

Excellent Household Beer

1 Bushel of malt and ½ a lb of hops to every 20 gallons of water [26]

The Hutchinson method of ensuring that their home brews were crystal clear was:

To fine beer, wine or Cider and to recover either when sour
The whites and Shells of 12 Eggs 1oz Salt of tartar, ½oz Pearl
ashes, ½oz grains of paradise bruised fine, and mix with as much

powder of Chalk as will make it the consistency of paste, roll this
into small balls, which put into the bung hole and stop down
immediately. This preparation will render the liquor fine, mild
and pleasant in a few days [27]

The only brewing recipe in Mary's notebook is not for anything
we would recognise as ale today. It comprised a solution flavoured
with elderflowers, raisins and gooseberries fermented to produce a
sparkling wine:

Ale Mearnce

30lb of Sugar 10 Gals of Water boiled ¾ hour & when milk warm
put in 5 qts of Elder flowers nicely picked from the stalks, then add
one gill of yeast; stir it twice a day till the flowers turn brown then
put it thro. a seive & let it stand a day or two. cask it and put in
6lb of chopped Raisins & a pint of the juice of green gooseberries,
cover it up and let it stand six months try it & if not quite bright
rack it off and dissolve an oz of Isinglass & 1lb of loaf sugar, stop it
& let it stand 2 months longer. [28]

> *1pt/600ml elderflowers, picked from the stalks, or*
> *1pt/600ml elderflower pressé*
> *9oz/250g chopped raisins   1 sachet/7g dried wine yeast*
> *4tbs gooseberry [or lemon] juice]   3lb/1·3kg sugar*

Bring 10pt/6l of water to the boil in a large pan, stir in
the sugar until dissolved, then allow to cool to 36°C, 95°F,
before stirring in the elderflowers or pressé, and the
yeast beaten into a little of the liquid until dissolved, and
then mixed into the remainder. Cover, and keep at room
temperature for about 4 days for the initial fermentation
to take place. Transfer into demijohns, add the raisins and
gooseberry juice, fit an air-lock, and leave in a cool place for
6 months before bottling.

Wine was not being drunk at Dove Cottage in 1801, but by Christmas
1802 Dorothy was able to tell her brothers that 'I continue to drink
wine though not in so large a quantity as I did. I find myself stronger
and better for it, but I hope in the summer I shall be able to leave it off
again.'[29] She clearly considered it to be more of a tonic than a luxury,
later becoming concerned that her sister-in-law Mary was not taking

sufficient to maintain good health. 'We cannot persuade her to drink wine [and she] will never take a glass except when we have company, and we always find that she looks better and is stronger when she has been obliged to drink wine for a week or a fortnight together.'[30] Wine was certainly offered to house-guests and those who came to dine, as in every middle-class household, and bottles were opened whenever a suitable opportunity arose.

Some wines would be obtained through the usual dealers, but never by the following method described by Coleridge:

> Receipt for brewing Wine
> Get two strong faithful men by proper Instruments – Vide
> Thieve's Calendar – break into a Wine Merchants Cellar –
> carry off a hogshead of best Claret or other as arbitrium –
> given me by Mrs Danvers – expertae crede.[31]

Others were received as gifts, Mary apparently acting as her own butler to ensure that the contents were safely transferred from cask to bottle at the appropriate time. In July 1828, for example, she wrote to Edward Quillinan to confirm the arrival of his wine, now 'safe in the Cellar and I look forward to no pleasant job in the bottling of it.' Five months later, sufficiently settled and matured, it was found 'excellent, then being bottled and laid down for future use'.[32] Home-made country wines were also drunk. At Dorothy's birthday party on Christmas Day, 1817, for example, the assembled company toasted her with a bottle of cowslip.[33] Mary, being rather abstemious, was a little shocked, however, when her student son William asked for cowslip wine to drink with his Sunday dinner during his visit from Oxford University in September, 1820.[34]

It is probable that the Wordsworths adopted country-wine-making practices from the Hutchinson sisters, who appear to have had considerable expertise in this field. Evidence for this comes from Mary's recipe book which includes instructions for making her gooseberry wine. This would use up some of their annual home-grown crop:

[Gooseberry Wine]

3 Gallons of red & green Gooseberries 3 do. Water previously boiled & cooled 10½lb of Lump sugar; the Gooseberries must be broken small & remain 2 days in the water stirred frequently. The sugar to be added to the Liquor when separated from the fruit

& put into the barrel as soon as dissolved. The Barrel must be rinsed with Brandy: it must be stirred every day for a fortnight then stopped down. The colour is best when the greater part of the berries is red. To be tapped about Xmas If not bright rinse the cask and put it in again with a little Isinglass dissolved in the wine.[35]

This is clearly copied from the same original source as the following, which comes from Joanna Hutchinson's recipe book:

Gooseberry Wine (Mrs Kis ...)

Take three gallons of Red and Green Gooseberries, three Gallons of Water previously boiled and cooled, 10½lbs of lump sugar, the Gooseberries must be broken small and pour in two days in the water stirred frequently. The Sugar to be added to the Liquor when separated from the fruit and put into a Barrel as soon as dissolved. The Barrel must be rinsed with Brandy: it must be stirred every day for a fortnight then stopped up. To be tapped about Xmas. If not bright rinse the Cask and put it in again with a little Isinglass in some of yr. Wine[36]

As the following recipes show, Joanna was making wines from ginger, raisins and wild flowers, including cowslips.

Ginger Wine ... Mrs Powell

5 Gallons of water 12lbs Lisbon sugar, the rinds of 12 lemons ¼lb Ginger bruised, boil and skim it, when cool put to it a little yeast on toasted bread and the next day put it in the cask with 1lb of chopped raisins to each gallon, a little isinglass and the juice of 12 lemons[37]

Ginger Wine

Take 6 Galls of water & 12lb Sugar, ½lb of Ginger bruised, put it in a bag & boil it ½ an hour in the water with the Sugar & whites of 4 Eggs, pour it upon the juice & Rinds of 9 Lemons, when cold put to it a little Beer yeast, let it work a day or two, then put it into the cask with the Ginger, Rinds, and a little Isinglass.[38]

Ginger Wine (Mr. Joy's receipt)

To 9 Galls of Water 18lbs of Sugar, boil them together for half an hour, taking off the scum as it rises, pour it into a Tub, when cold put to it as much good yeast as you think will work it, let it stand 3 days, put into the barrel 1lb of Ginger Bruised, the rinds of 18 Seville Oranges & as many Lemons pared thin, the pulp of the Oranges & Lemons beat up with as much sugar as will make it very sweet & 2lbs of Raisins stoned, 1 qt. of Brandy, ½ oz of Isinglass cut small, pour the fermenting Liquor upon these Ingredients, when it has done working stop it up close & let it stand ½ year before it is drawn off. [39]

Raisin Wine

Put 7lbs of Malaga Raisins to every Gal of cold Spring Water, after standing for 3 days, draw as much off as will boil ¼lb Hops for a qr. of an hour, which must be put all together boiling hot into the Cask, leave the Bung open till done fermenting, close the Cask about 2 Months when it will be fit for drinking. [40]

Raisin Wine [Tho King]

To 7lb of Raisins, stalks & all, put one Gall. of cold spring Water, put them into a Hogshead, according to the Quantity you wish to make, allowing room for the swelling of the fruit & stirrings, which must be done every other Day for a Month, stop it close & let it stand on the fruit 10 or 12 Months. Draw the liquor from the fruit into a clean cask, take care that the Cask be full, to every 10 Galls. of Wine put one pint of Brandy. Let it remain in the Cask six Months or as long as you think proper. Fine it with blue Milk, to 10 Gallons one pint to be put in to the Cask at the time you draw it from the fruits. The sort of Raisins [& ?] are the Lexia, any other sort perhaps may do as well. [41]

Smyrna [Raisin] Wine (Mr Joy's receipt)

Boil the quantity of water wanted & when cold put in 8lbs of Fruit [Smyrna raisins] to the Gal. Let it stand a fortnight in a Tub & stir it 2 or 3 times a day. Then put all into the Barrel & stir it once a day till it has done working, which will be perhaps a fortnight or 3 weeks, it should not stand longer. Take it out of the Barrel & press the liquor from the fruit, then fill the Barrel full that it may again ferment out of the cask, & let it remain till that is over, take out as much wine as you put in Brandy (nearly 1 Gall to 18 of wine) add a Gill of skimmed Milk with a little Isinglass dissolved in wine & the whites of 2 or 3 Eggs. It may stand in the Cask [& ?] a year [42]

Cowslip Wine

To 20qts. of Water 15lbs of Sugar, & rather more than 1 qt. of picked Cowslips to each qt. Boil the water with the Sugar ½ an Hour, put in the whites & shells of 6 Eggs well beaten, skim it, and when nearly cold pour it upon the Cowslips & 6 Lemons skins & pared, let it stand all night, then put to it a Gill of Yeast & for 24 Hours stir it frequently, then put it in the cask with a little Isinglass dissolved in vinegar. [43]

Elderflower Wine [Mrs King]

Take 30lbs of Lump Sugar, 10 Gallons of Water (Ale measure) boiled ¾ of an Hour, and when Milk warm put 5 pts of Elderflowers nicely picked from the stalks, then add ¼ of a pint of yeast: stir it twice a day till the flowers turn brown, then put it through a sieve & let it stand a Day or two. Cask it & put in 6lb of chopped Raisins & a pint of the juice of Green Gooseberries. Close it up & let it stand for 6 Months, try it & if not very bright rack it off & dissolve an Ounce of Isinglass to a lb of lump Sugar, put that in, stop it & let it stand 2 Months longer. [44]

Clary is a herb found mainly in the south of England, which explains the use of its violet or white flowers in this recipe of the Fricker family:

Clary Wine

To 10 gallons of water, 1 peck of Clary flowers, 2lb & ½ or a little more (but not quite 3lbs) of Loaf Sugar to each gallon, boil the sugar and water, clear it with white of eggs, when cold put it into a barrel with a square hole at the top with a little yeast, when it begins to work put in the flowers and stir it twice a day for a

*fortnight, then add a little Isinglass and bung it up. Bottle it in
3 or 4 months. The Barrel may be kept from year to year with the
flowers in it. measure the flowers lightly, 8 quarts to the peck.[45]*

While staying overnight at Hawes at the head of Wensleydale in early
October 1802, the Wordsworths enjoyed the evening with 'a shilling's
worth of negus'.[46] This blend of port or sherry, sugar, flavouring and
hot water had been invented by Colonel Francis Negus about a century
earlier, but was still very popular throughout the country:

Negus

2-3 lumps of sugar
4 fl oz/ 100 ml port or sherry
1 lemon   *pinch of grated nutmeg*

Rub the sugar on the lemon rind to extract the oils, put
this in a ½pt/300ml heatproof glass, add the port, and fill
up with boiling water. Stir to dissolve the sugar and finish
with a sprinkling of nutmeg.[47]

In the heat of a spring day in May 1802, William and Dorothy,
accompanied by Coleridge, dined 'upon a moss-covered Rock, rising
out of the bed of the River' at what is now Thirlmere. Here she 'drank a
little Brandy and water and was in Heaven'.[48] Brandy, and particularly
rum, were both popular in the Lakes, much being smuggled into
the prosperous port of Whitehaven. On 1st September, 1800, the
Wordsworths 'borrowed some bottles for bottling rum' from their
friends the Simpsons.[49] These may have been of glass or perhaps 'grey
hens', the imported salt-glazed bottles used for ale and spirits on the
local farms. Dark rum can be a fiery liquor in the mouth and throat,
but these properties could be remarkably transformed by adding sugar,
lemon juice and lemon zest to produce 'shrub'. English travellers had
first come across 'Scherab or Persian wine' in the mid seventeenth
century, but its popularity here really started in the 1740s. It has a
decidedly citrus flavour, its high alcohol content being detected more
by a quickening pulse and a warm glow rather than by its deceptively
mild taste.

Shrub

4qts of Lemon juice, 4lbs lump Sugar, 9 or 10 qts of Spirits. Pare the Lemons very thin & infuse the Peel in half of the spirit 24 Hours, then put all into a Cask, tumble it twice a day till the Sugar is dissolved, put into the Cask the white of 2 Eggs let it stand till fine, then Bottle it.[50]

1pt/600ml rum	*4oz/100g sugar*
6 lemons	*white of 1 egg*

Use a potato peeler to pare the zest from the lemons, then squeeze them into a measuring jug, to produce ½pt/300ml juice. Strain this through a fine sieve or a piece of muslin into a large jar, add the zest, rum and sugar, seal the jar, and shake it from time to time over two days, by which time the sugar should have dissolved, and the zest given up its oils.

Strain the liquid to remove the zest, beat the egg white thoroughly, with a little of the liquid, beat this into the remainder, leave for two hours, then pass through a coffee filter-paper which has been freshly rinsed in cold water. Pour the first few cloudy tablespoonfuls back into the filter paper, after which it will run through crystal clear over the next couple of days, when it can be bottled for use as a liqueur.

The final recipe in this section is for an extremely useful winter-time drink, blackcurrant vinegar. On 22nd April, 1802, Coleridge accompanied the Wordsworths on a walk up Easedale, where the whole party was drenched. After returning to dinner at Dove Cottage Dorothy and Coleridge 'drank black currants and water'.[51] Since fresh, ripe blackcurrants are only in season between July and August, they must have used this simple, sharp-flavoured cordial made up with hot water, to enjoy this most comfortable remedy for colds and chills:

Blackcurrant vinegar

Fill a jar with black currants, then pour in as much vinegar as the jars will hold; let it stand 4 days, stirring it well each day Then squeeze out the fruit & pass the liquor thro' a canvas bag to every pint of juice put a lb. of Loaf sugar, let it simmer ½ an hour, when cold bottle it for use

N.B. very good for colds. Raspberry vinegar may be made the same way.[52]

Chapter Eleven

OF PACE EGGS

Eggs have provided a potent symbol of the resurrection of Christ at Eastertime for many centuries. In Martindale they were collected by the priest as his Easter dues. During the sixty-seven years of his incumbency Richard Birkett used a piece of wood with a hole in it as a gauge, returning to each farmer all those which were so small as to pass through.[1]

In the opening decades of the nineteenth century it was customary for children in the Lake District to give 'pace eggs' to their friends, this name being derived from 'paschal', relating to Easter. Each egg was decorated to the utmost of the giver's skill, one method being to dip it in hot water for a few moments, then use the tip of a tallow candle to inscribe an appropriate name or date. This acted as a resist, the lines remaining white in contrast to the background, which readily absorbed colour when immersed in a pan of hot dye. Writing in 1825, 'Mr J.B.' of Maryport described how:

> Another method of ornamenting 'pace eggs' is, however, much neater, although more laborious, than that with the tallow-candle. The egg being dyed, it may be decorated in a very pretty manner, by means of a penknife, with which the dye may be scraped off, leaving the design white, on a coloured ground. The egg is frequently divided into compartments, which are filled up according to the taste and skill of the designer. Generally one compartment contains the name (being young and unsophisticated) also the age of the party for whom the egg is intended. In another is, perhaps, a landscape; and sometimes a cupid is found lurking in a third; so that these 'pace-eggs' become very useful auxiliaries to the missives of St Valentine. Nothing was more common in the childhood of the writer, than to see a number of these eggs preserved very carefully in the corner cupboard; each egg being the occupant of a deep, long-stemmed ale-glass, through which the inscription could be read without removing it. Probably

many of these eggs now remain in Cumberland, which
would afford as good evidence of dates in a court of justice,
as a tombstone or a family bible.[2]

One of the finest of all egg decorators was James Dixon who started
work as the Wordsworths' gardener sometime before 1829. He was
a much-loved servant, remaining at Rydal Mount as long as it was
inhabited by any member of the family, and regularly visiting their
graves to the end of his life. He was later remembered as 'yan they
called Dixon, smart lile chap as iver was seen in these parts, but ter'ble
given over to cold watter and temperance he woz. Coomed out of a
union [a workhouse], but verra neat, and always a word for onybody,
and a verra quiet man, particular quiet, nivver up to nea mischief, and
always sat at heam wi' t' lasses a mending and sewing o' evenings ye
kna.'[3] In 1830 Sarah Hutchinson described him as:

> our industrious and simple-hearted Serving-man James,
> who can do all sorts of little jobs, mend chair-bottoms,
> weave garden nets, make mats, list sheets etc., etc., has
> made cap stands for the Ladies of this house & By the Bye,
> his wedding present to Mrs. J.W. Was a paste-pin turned by
> himself, and a potato bruiser both made of wood grown in
> Rydal Mount Grounds.[4]

He was also a skilled gardener, even though:

> He knew nothing of gardening when he came to us but
> kindly took to the work; and is now even passionately
> attached to the gardens especially the ornamental part
> as my Sister [Mary] says he worships his flowers . Every
> morning from her bed-room window does she see him
> going his Rounds and standing over every particular Plant
> that pleases his family & His health is delicate and he could
> not stand hard exercise.[5]

From these accounts, it is obvious that he combined a real appreciation
of the beauties of nature with considerable ingenuity and dexterous
craftsmanship. Even so, the exceptionally high quality of the design
and execution demonstrated in his decorated pace eggs still comes as a
complete revelation. The Wordsworth Trust at Dove Cottage preserves
a number of those he made for William's grandchildren between 1868

and 1878. Compared to any other English examples, they are truly magnificent, standing at least equal to the very best in the whole of Europe.[6] He also decorated Easter eggs, conkers and snail shells, some being the treasured possessions of local families whose great-great-grandfathers received them as presents from him when he used to visit Langdale School in 1863.[7]

Unlike many other local egg-decorators, who used either natural materials or pieces of cloth with non-fast dyes to colour their eggs, James Dixon appears to have used the strongest of commercially-manufactured dyes or inks to achieve the richest of royal blues, purples, red-browns or blacks. Using a sharp-pointed blade, he then scratched through this layer to reveal the white shell beneath. Some of his eggs demonstrate an amazing degree of geometric accuracy, dividing their curving surfaces into tiny squares, or circular panels, while others are in much freer, but still well-balanced and highly detailed designs. These include swans, poultry and wild birds, as well as sprays of foliage and flowers informed by his occupation as a gardener. Without doubt, these are among the most important examples of English folk-art, always intended to be preserved and displayed, unlike most other locally-decorated examples.

It was during James Dixon's time that a remarkable distribution of pace eggs took place at Rydal Mount. The date was Tuesday 9th April, 1844, Wordsworth's 74th birthday, when a celebratory fête was provided by Miss Isabella Fenwick, a close family friend then living in Ambleside.

> 'The Grasmere boys and girls came first, and took their places on the benches placed around the gravelled part of the esplanade; their eyes fixed with wonder and admiration on the tables covered with oranges, gingerbread and painted eggs, ornamented with daffodils, laurels, and moss, gracefully intermixed & Neighbours, old and young, of all degrees, ascended to the Mount & and every face looked friendly and happy. Each child brought its own mug, and held it out to be filled with tea, in which ceremony all assisted. Large baskets of currant cakes were handed round and liberally dispensed; and as each detachment of children had satisfied themselves with tea and cake, they were moved off, to play hide and seek among the evergreens on the grassy part of the Mount & The children, who amounted altogether to above 300, gave

three cheers to Mr. Wordsworth and Miss F[enwick]. After some singing and dancing, and after the division of eggs, gingerbread and oranges had taken place, we all began to disperse.[8]

The pace eggs intended to be given away to children calling at farmhouse and cottage doors on Good Friday were either simply dyed or dotted with tallow to present a piebald or bird's-eye appearance. Made by the younger boys who had still to aspire to motifs such as Cupid's bent bow and quiverful of arrows, a flaming torch or a heart and a true-lover's knot, their dyes were brown onion skins, green ivy leaves, yellow gorse flowers etc.[9] Often the children would arrive in a small group, perhaps dressed in character, those of the mid-nineteenth century appearing as Lord Nelson, Jolly Jack Tar, Old Tosspot and a female Old Muse with her bags. They started their performance with the traditional chant of:

Here's two or three jolly boys all of one mind,
We've come a pace-egging, I hope you'll prove kind,
I hope you'll prove kind, with your eggs and strong beer,
And we'll come no more nigh you until the next year.

Each character then stepped forward and exclaimed its particular line, after which the resident 'Ladies and gentlemen that sits by the fire' were requested to put their hands in their pockets and remember that it was pace-egging time.[10]

On Easter Monday the children disposed of their eggs in various ways, either tossing them in the air, rolling them down a particular local hill, or trundling them, as at Kendal.[11] Here pairs of children sat at each side of a piece of level turf and rolled their eggs so as to collide in the middle, until one was broken and forfeited to the winner, who probably gobbled it up immediately. Alternatively a child holding an egg in one hand would challenge another to give it a blow with his egg, the one that survived being given the title of a cock of one, two, three etc.[12] Unfortunately there are few early records of these customs in the Lake District, since they were probably so well-known that no one ever thought it worthwhile to mention them, but they formed an essential event in the annual cycle of celebrations. Egg-rolling was still practised in some villages into at least the 1950s, and egg decorating still continues as a hobby, but rarely, if ever, to James Dixon's remarkable standards.

Chapter Twelve

OF HOME REMEDIES

I n common with most other personal recipe books, those of the Wordsworth, Hutchinson and Fricker families include practical remedies for alleviating minor medical conditions, as well as for coping with a variety of housekeeping problems. None of them should be used today, but they are reproduced here for their general interest, and to shed light on the ways in which the families dealt with ailments partly resulting from their particular lifestyles.

Dorothy's journal mentions that meals were occasionally missed due to unspecified illnesses, their appetites usually being quite good. However, the remedies recorded in Mary's recipe book suggest that they sometimes needed to modify their digestions:

Tonic for the Stomach

½oz red rose leaves
¼oz snepe root
¼oz bit. orange Peel
pour on the above 1qt. of boiling water. 2 in ye Day [1]

[The 'snepe root' may possibly be snake root, Polygale senega or Aristolchia serpentaria].

The Frickers, meanwhile, used a hop solution:

To create an Appetite

Put a handfull of Hops into a quart jug & pour boiling water on it with a little ginger [2]

Laxatives were apparently also in demand, the Wordsworths making up both Daffy's Elixir, a highly-regarded tonic invented by Anthony Daffy around 1680, and a mixture of heira picra (a compound of purgative aloes and wind-expelling cinnamon) and a starchy gelling agent called saloop:

Daffy's elixir

1½oz Rhubarb 1½ Senna
1lb Raisins shred 1oz figs sliced
1oz Liquorice sliced & scraped
1oz Cummin seeds
½ Dram Cochineal bruised
Do Saffron
infuse in 3 pints of brandy 8 days strain it off & put on 3 pints
more let this infuse 8 days longer pour it off & mix all together [3]

Mrs Hugessen

1oz Heira Picra
1 Do Salap to a bottle of White Wine – let it stand 6 weeks sheking
the bottle often – strain it - & add a glass of brandy – Dose ½ a
wine Glass with water. [4]

Joanna Hutchinson had a recipe for a similar purgative compound
which included Castile soap:

Mrs Hugesson's Pills

Rhubarb and Ipicacuanha each ½ dram, Castle Soap 1 dram in
30 Pills [5]

while Martha Fricker recommended:

A Saline Draught

½ an oz of nitre to a pint of toast & water [6]

Even more troublesome complaints were treated with self-
prescribed remedies. To dull the raging agony of her toothache,
Dorothy sometimes dosed herself with laudanum, a strong opiate,
for example.[7] Meanwhile the pile-wort (Ranunculus Ficaria or Ficaria
verna) which 'spread out on the grass a thousand shining stars' of
glossy yellow flowers in the garden at Dove Cottage, was probably used
to heal William's piles.[8]

Even for people who were born and bred in the Lake District, the
cold of the winter months presented a real challenge. Out of doors,
especially with a hard frost and a biting wind, it could take the breath

away, and it wasn't much better inside, except within the immediate radiance of the fireplace. After one February night in 1802 Dorothy described how: 'At first I went to bed I seemed to be warm, I suppose because the cold air, which I had just left, no longer touched my body, but I soon found that I was mistaken, I could not sleep for sheer cold.'[9] Only those who can remember sleeping in the usually sub-zero temperatures of pre-centrally heated winter bedrooms can fully appreciate her experience, and the symptoms it produced. Chilblains were a regular seasonal problem, tender and itchy inflammations on hands and feet exposed to the cold, which could easily degenerate into ulcers. To cure them Dorothy used this plaster:

For Chilblains

1oz Rosin 1 Do Bees wax 1 Do Lard, 2 Spoonful Sweet oil to be simmered in a new pimpkin. The feet to be washed, a plaister of this mixture to be spread thinly and applied fresh every third night.[10]

while Joanna Hutchinson recommended several others.

For Chilblains

one oz of White Copperas [zinc proto-sulphate] dissolved in a quart of water. This application must be used before they break [11]

Chilblains

Citrine ointment 1oz, oil of turpentine 2 Drachms, oil of olive 4 Drachms, mixed, to be well rubbed in night & morning.[12]

Do. Sir Astley Cooper

1oz of Camphorated Spirit of wine, ½oz of the liquor of subacetate of lead. Mix and apply 3 or 4 times a day [13]

[Chilblains]

1oz White Copperas in a qt. of Water will remove Chilblains [14]

Boils, infected wounds and gatherings were treated with salves which both helped to extract puss etc., and soothed and healed the inflammation. Of their effective ingredients, diachalum was a compound of lead oxide, boiled with olive oil and water to form a stiff paste. These recipes come from one of Dorothy's commonplace books, probably of the later 1820s:

Miss Barker's White Salve

Diachalum ½lb sweet oil 4oz (¼ pint) Chalk 4oz Vinegar 4oz
Cut the Diachalum into thin slices put into a new glazed pipkin
with the oil melt gently over a fire Add the Chalk finely powdered
& sifted, stirring till cold
Drawing Salve Do.
Millicot plaster 4oz Sweet oil 3oz
Melt by the fire
To be put on a bit of Lint, & to be applied to the & of a Boil or
Sore with a plaster of the White Salve above it. When sufficiently
drawn, the White Salve only is wanted.[15]

In addition to chilblains, the winter months also brought on coughs and colds, for which medicines were made up to recipes such as these:

Cough Mixture

1oz Elixir of Panegoric
1oz of Syrup of Poppies
½oz Sweet nitre
½oz Gum Arabic
These ingredients to be well mixed and a teaspoonful taken two or
three times a day [16]

For a Cough & cold

one drachm of Elixir of Vitriol & drachms of Laudanum, 3
teaspoonfulls full of honey, 30 drops of mixture to be taken three
times a day [17]

The Elixir of Panegoric was a camphorated tincture of opium with aniseed and benzoic acid, the laudanum also being an opiate, while the Elixir of Vitriol was aromatic sulphuric acid. Their sharp flavours were masked and soothed by the use of either the opiate syrup of poppies or the honey, but even so it would have been unwise to have taken these medicines for more than a short period.

The only remedy for a childhood illness to be recorded in the Wordsworth recipes is one for croup, which Dorothy noted down from the *Morning Chronicle* probably about the time of young John Wordsworth's birth in 1803. This disease caused inflammation of the larynx and windpipe, as well as a characteristic sharp, ringing cough, and frequently proved fatal. Since the mixture of camphor and sal ammoniac (ammonium chloride) could not be applied directly to the affected parts, they were both dissolved in volatile distilled spirits of wine. When applied to the external skin of the throat, either directly or on a piece of flannel, they were rapidly evaporated and inhaled, just like the medicinal vapour-rubs popular up to the mid twentieth century.

For the Croup   Ward's Essence

4oz of the best highly rectified Spirits of Wine 4oz Camphor to be thoroughly mixed & incorporated then add 4oz of the best soluble Sal Ammoniac.

If both the Spirits be not good the proper quantity of Camphor will not be taken up by them.

Tried by Dr Hawkins of Monmouthshire with good success. The throat to be bathed with the Essence & a piece of flannel to be dipped with it, & tied round.[18]

At a time when it was more usual to walk than to ride, it was essential to keep the feet in good condition, partly by using well-fitting footwear, and partly by treating corns etc. before they caused major problems. The Wordsworths used this remedy:

Bath for the feet

Muriacic Acid 2 of each
Warm water 3 gallons
The two acids to be added each separately to ½ a pint cold water & then mixed together, by the Druggist. Then put to 3 galls. warm water Feet to be kept in ¼ an hour at bed time every night. If a proper strength it lasts like & ?[19]

Unfortunately the recipe gives only one of the two acids. Muriacic acid is the now obsolete name for hydrochloric acid, which explains why the Wordsworths preferred to have their druggist carry out its initial mixing and dilution. Joanna Hutchinson's recipe used, as a safer alternative, a strong lye made by dissolving willow ashes in vinegar to soften both:

Warts & Corns

The bark of the Willow tree burnt to ashes and [mixed?] with strong Vinegar form a [& ?] which effectively eradicate by repeated application warts, corns, and all cutaneous excrescences [20]

For complaints which affected the limbs and joints rather than the feet, her remedies include:

Oliver's Oil for Sprains &

Hungary Water 2 ounces, Powers of Amber 2 do. Spirits of Lavendar 1 Dram, Spirit of Wine 4 ounces Spirit of Nitre, sweet, 1 Dram Tincture of Saffron 10 drops
Mix
For inward Bruises 8 to 10 drops taken twice a day [21]

The following remedy for rheumatism which was based on mustard, which the Wordsworths obtained from 'the Cockermouth traveller', a woman who called at Dove Cottage on her way to Ulverston, carrying her dry goods on her back, and planning to return in time for Ambleside Fair. [22]

For Rheumatism

Take of the best Durham Mustard seed 3 oz, boil it gently in three pints of water till reduced to one, then add one pint of skimmed Milk & strain it through a sieve, one Teacupful of warm [taken] every night & morning. [23]

Spending so much time in the open air in all weathers took its toll on the complexion. In 1810 Russell's poem To a Lady described the best available means of easing the combined effects of wind, rain and cold:

'A pot of cold cream to Eliza you send.
Who'er with this cream shall her countenance smear,
All redness and roughness will strait disappear.' [24]

Joanna Hutchinson used this recipe:

To make Cold Cream

*Dissolve half a Cake of white wax in half a Pint of oil of sweet
Almonds, then put the whole into a large basonful of cold spring
water and beat it with a silver spoon for half an hour, change the
water and beat it again for half an hour longer, this water must
then be poured off and a quart of rosewater added in which it must
be beaten an hour, put it in cups, leaving sufficient room to cover it
with a little fresh rosewater, tie it close with paper.*[25]

One Friday in March 1802, as dusk was falling, Coleridge arrived at
Dove Cottage, having walked from Keswick via Dunmail Raise in
torrential rain. As Dorothy recorded in her journal,

> 'His eyes were a little swollen with the wind, I was much
> affected by the sight of him he seemed half stupified &
> Poor C! I did not wish for, or expect him, it rained so.'[26]

The long hours which both he and the Wordsworths spent at their
reading and writing, especially by candlelight or firelight during the
long winter evenings, also produced eye strain. Coleridge sometimes
had to work throughout the night to complete his essays for the
newspapers, for example, while Dorothy described many evenings
such as one in November 1801,

> 'all sitting by a nice fire. W. with his book and a candle and
> Mary writing to Sara'.[27]

Dorothy sometimes suffered problems with her eyes, as noted in her
letters, but they were rarely, if ever, as bad as William's.[28] His problems
were exacerbated with the smoke problems at Allan Bank, but
continued to increase over the following years. In 1837, for example, he
described how

> 'My eyes are not bad, but certainly weaker than I could
> wish, the eyelids reddening and the balls watering
> when exposed to strong light or sharp air, but very little
> bloodshot.[29]

This, it should be stressed, was when they were 'not bad'. This explains the presence of a number of home-made eye washes in Mary's recipe book:

Eye Water

2oz Rosemary Leaves
¼pt Port Wine
¼pt Water [30]
Eye Water
2 Dr. Borax
9qr vitriolated zinc
3oz rose or elder flower water [31]

Joanna Hutchinson's remedy was based on sassafras. This was a small elder-like tree, native to North America, whose bark was used as an alterative, restoring the organs to a healthy condition.

Sore Eyes

Take small sticks of salsafras split in 4 Pieces, put them in a Vessel with cold water, they impart a glutinous matter in the water, wash the Eyes with this Liquid & will cure without smarting or heals. [32]

Although not medicinal, the use of toilet soap was certainly necessary both for personal hygiene and for shaving. Camphor, whether prepared from the original Far Eastern shrub, or by the developing chemical industry, was a white, crystalline volatile substance, with a strong and very characteristic smell, which many people today still associate with mothballs.

Wash Balls

1lb of white Soap shaved fine 3d of Spermacete bruised & 3d Camphire dissolved in Spirit of Wine, 4d of the best sweet oil, put these ingredients into a jar & stir it till all is dissolved then take it off & continue stirring, till cold enough to make into Balls. [33]

The recipe books also contain instructions for keeping clothing and footwear in a good, presentable condition. Items of linen were relatively valuable, and so it was essential that each piece should be indelibly marked with the name of its owner, perhaps also with the date of its acquisition, and sometimes a number to relate it to a household inventory. Making the ink was a potentially dangerous operation:

To make ink for marking Linen

Pour a little nitric acid (aqua fortis) into a cup or glass and add to it a small piece of pure silver, when the effervescence ceases filter the solution through a piece of blotting paper, and put it into a small phial, then add to it a little gum arabic, and a little of the paint called Sap green, after the whole is perfectly combined and is fit for use [34]

Such an ink had to survive the repeated washings which usually improved the whiteness and texture of the linen. In contrast all wool, silk, velvets etc. had to be given some form of dry-cleaning, as washing could damage their surfaces. If dry-brushing or gentle sponging failed to remove stains, especially those of oily or waxy substances, the best treatment was to use a highly volatile ether:

Scouring Spirit

Pyreligneous Aether 1 ounce, essence of Lemons 3 drams, mix, the part should be well rubbed with Tow or woollen Cloth moistened with this Composition. [35]

For footwear, home-made liquid blackening was made by combining burnt ivory powder with an emulsion of vinegar, sulphuric acid (then known as oil of vitriol), olive oil and sugar. It was then stored in corked jars ready for use.

Blackening

4oz Ivory black, 2oz Coarse sugar mixed well with a quart of vinegar, add carefully ½oz Oil of vitriol stirring very well with a stick in a deep earthen vessel, last of all add two large spoonfuls of sweet oil. [36]

Much of the redecoration and maintenance of Dove Cottage was carried out by its occupants, rather than by local craftsmen. Repainting was best done in the summer months, when the longer days and warmer weather meant that the doors and windows could be left open to speed up the drying process. In June 1802 Dorothy made her start by actually grinding the paint, probably using a pestle and mortar to crush lumps of prepared chalk before mixing it to a thin creamy consistency with size, perhaps a bit of washing blue, and water. Next morning she used this to whitewash the ceiling, the effort leading her to spend the afternoon in bed. Her friend Miss Simpson then colourwashed the walls. [37]

The rubbing of the tables, or furniture polishing, appears to have been one of William's domestic chores, but the cleaning which most households carried out once a year involved washing off any accumulated dirt with vinegar before applying linseed oil. For mahogany, it was coloured red with the root of alkanet or Dyer's Bugloss (Anchusa or Alkenna tinctoria) and Rose Pink, a pigment made by dying whiting with red-purple Brazil-wood.

Clean Mahogany

First wash it clean with vinegar. Then take 4d. of Alkanet Root, 2d Rose Pink, 1 Pint of cold drawn nseed Oil. Put it into an Earthen pot & let it stand 24 Hours. Rub the Mahogany with this mixture, then after standing 24 hours rub it bright with a Linen Cloth. [38]

The next recipe comes from Mary Wordsworth's book. It is not domestic, however, but veterinary, describing how to make a plaster to cure warbles, the small hard tumours on a horse's back, caused by the pressure of the saddle, particularly if this area was not kept perfectly clean. She was an accomplished horsewoman, riding sidesaddle in a habit in her younger days, and probably learned simple vetinary cures of this kind while living at Sockburn and at Gallow Hill.

Warbles or sore back of a Horse

Com. Pitch [&] Pitch ea 3oz
Mastic[&] Francincence ea 1oz
Common Turpentine, Galbarum [&] Bole Armeriac ½oz
Powder the Bole armeriac & mix it with the other ingredients when melted over a gentle fire.
This plaster is to be spread on soft Leather & remain on the part till well. [39]

The final recipe is by far the most appropriate for the household of a major poet, and for one in which writing was such an important everyday occupation. It is Dorothy's instructions for making ink, written in the early years at Dove Cottage, and most probably used to make the ink with which William's finest poetry was first set down on paper.

To make Ink

an ounce of Gum arabick, 30 [oak] Galls, 1oz sulphate of iron. A wine quart of water of which put as much upon the Gum as will dissolve it & the rest on the Galls & iron. Let it stand 3 days without cork shake it after three days add the gum & it is fit for use.[40]

As this chapter clearly demonstrates, a considerable degree of training and expertise was required in order to manage even modest households. Compared to our current lifestyles, which enjoy ready access to every conceivable ready-made commodity, those of most country housewives and housekeepers of the early nineteenth century were amazingly self-sufficient. Medicines, cosmetics, cleaning materials, paints and polishes were all made up in the kitchen from a selection of raw materials, following traditions established by generations of trial and error experiences. Today they not only impress us with their comprehensive range of solutions to all manner of practical problems, but they also help us to comprehend otherwise intangible aspects of the everyday lives of the poets. These might include the almond and rosewater scents from their cold cream, the mothball smell from their wash-balls, or the heavy odour of linseed after furniture polishing. In the storecupboards we may also trace the aromas of rose petals, orange peel, liquorice, cummin, saffron, lavender, rosewater and elderflower water, along with those of the more dangerous acids and chemicals used to ease the symptoms of various illnesses and complaints.

It is extremely fortunate that Mary Wordsworth, her sister Joanna Hutchinson, and Coleridge and Southey's sister-in-law Martha Fricker all recorded so many of their recipes in their manuscript notebooks, and that these are now preserved by the Wordsworth Trust at Dove Cottage. Without them our knowledge of their lives, and also our ability to make and taste so many of their authentic dishes, would have been totally impossible.

APPENDIX

Table-Linen at Dove Cottage

One month after Mary's arrival at Grasmere as William's wife, a list was drawn up of all the linen which Mary's family had provided for her new home. It is interesting both for its content, and for the initials marking the origin of each piece. For centuries it had been the practice for families to grow their own flax, scotch and spin it into yarn, have it converted into cloth by a local weaver, and then make it up into sheets, tablecloths, towels, shirts, underwear etc. as required. Such pieces would then be handed down through successive generations, being extremely hard-wearing. This is shown by the initial marking each of Mary's linens:

G	Gamage
H	Hutchinson
JH	John Hutchinson (1736-1785) her father
MC	Margaret Cooper, her grandmother's niece
MM	Margaret Monkhouse (1717-1788) her grandmother
WM	Monkhouse (1746- 1809) her maternal uncle

The linen was made of distinctive weaves and yarns, the finest being damask, in which the loom was set to produce elaborate borders and patterns which absorbed or reflected the light on the otherwise uniformly white surface of the material. Next came diaper, a twill weave giving a small all-over diamond pattern, hence the American term 'dyper' for the English 'nappy'. Huckaback was usually thicker, with a chequerboard pattern, its absorbency making it suitable for hand-towels, as well as other uses. Mary's probably came from Darlington, the major national centre for its production. Finally, there was plain-woven linen, where the quality was largely dependent on the fineness of the yarn, anything from the almost transparent lawn to the roughest of coarse cloths. In addition to bedlinen and towels, this is the account of Mary's linen which came from Penrith to Grasmere in November 1802 (original spellings corrected):

1 small Damask Table Cloth
1 large Do
2 Diaper Table Cloths 1 marked WM the other unmarked
1 old Diaper, Do
2 Diaper Breakfast cloths one marked H the other unmarked
2 large Huckaback Table Cloths marked H
1 Do Do JH
2 coarse & strong, one marked G the other unmarked
3 breakfast Do

With a total of fifteen tablecloths to choose from, she could always provide a suitable cloth for any meal, fine damask for formal entertaining, diaper or huckaback for friends etc., and coarse and strong for everyday use.

BIBLIOGRAPHY

Anon., *15 Books of Old Recipes as used by the Pease and Gurney Households in the XVIIIth Century* (Newcastle upon Tyne c. 1910)

Bradley, R., *The Country Housewife and Lady's Director II* (1732)

Brears, P., 'Traditional Food in the Lake Counties', in Wilson, C.A., *Traditional Food East and West of the Pennines* (Edinburgh 1991)

Bowness, W., *Rustic Sketches* (1868)

Brown, P.B., *In Praise of Hot Liquors* (York 1995)

Coleridge, S.T., *The Notebooks of, I 1794-1804* ed. Coburn, K. (1957-62)

De Quincey, T., *Recollections of the Lake Poets* (Harmondsworth 1985)

Dickinson, W., *The Dialect of Cumberland* (1878)

Dods, M., *The Cook and Housekeeper's Manual* (Edinburgh 1829, reprinted 1988)

Farley, J., *The London Art of Cookery* (1793, reprinted Lewes 1988)

Fell, J., 'Some Illustrations of Home Life in Lonsdale North of the Sands in the 17th and 18th Centuries', *Trans. Cumb. & West. Arch. Soc. XI* (Kendal 1891)

Glasse, H., *The Art of Cookery Made Plain and Easy* (1747)

Griggs, E.L., *Collected Letters of Samuel Taylor Coleridge* (Oxford 1956-71)

Hart, K., *Dove Cottage* (1966)

Holmes, R., *Coleridge, Early Visions* (Sevenoaks 1989)

Hone, W., *The Everyday Book* (1826-7)

Howe, H.W., *Greta Hall, Home of Coleridge and Southey* (Norfolk 1977)

Hutchinson, Sara, *Letters of*, ed. Coburn, K. (Toronto 1954)

Kipling, C., 'Charr, a Northern Fish', *Petit Propos Culinaires, 17* (Totnes 1984)

Lee, E., *Dorothy Wordsworth* (1894)

McCracken, D., *Wordsworth & the Lake District* (Oxford 1985)

Moorman, M., *William Wordsworth: I The Early Years, II The Later Years* (Oxford 1957)

Newall, V., *An Egg at Easter* (1971)

Nicholson, N., *The Lake District* (Harmondsworth 1982)

Nott, J., *The Cooks and Confectioners Dictionary* (1726)

Raffald, E., *The Experienced English Housekeeper* (1769, reprinted Lewes 1997)

Rawnsley, E.F., *Grasmere in Wordsworth's Time* (Kendal n.d.)

Rawnsley, H.D., *Reminiscences of Wordsworth among the Peasantry of Westmoreland*, intro. by Tillotson, G., (1968)

Rundell, M.E., *A New System of Domestic Cookery* (1813)

Rollinson, W., *Life and Traditions in the Lake District* (1974)

Stead, J., 'Prodigal Frugality: Yorkshire Pudding and Parkin', in Wilson, C.A., *Traditional Food East and West of the Pennines* (Edinburgh 1991)

Sullivan, J., *Cumberland and Westmorland Ancient and Modern* (London & Kendal 1852)

Thompson, T.W., *Wordsworth's Hawkshead* (Oxford 1970)

White, F., *Good Things in England* (1974)

Wordsworth, C., *Memoirs of William Wordsworth* (1851)

Wordsworth, Dorothy, *Journal*, ed. Moorman, M., (Oxford 1971)

Wordsworth, Mary, *Letters of, 1800-1855*, ed. Burton, E., (Oxford 1958)

Wordsworth, William, *Guide to the Lakes*, ed. De Sélincourt, (2004)

Wordsworth, William & Dorothy, *Letters of;* ed. De Sélincourt

   The Early Years 1787-1805, (Oxford 1967)

   The Middle Years 1806-1811,(Oxford 1969)

   The Middle Years part 2, 1812-1820, (Oxford 1970)

   The Later Years part 1 1821-1828, (Oxford 1979)

   The Later Years part 2 1829-1834 (Oxford 1979)

   The Later Years part 3 1835-1839 (Oxford 1979)

   The Later Years part 4 1840-1853 (Oxford 1979)

   A Supplement of New Letters, ed. Hill, H.G.. (Oxford 1993)

Wondrausch, M., 'Char' in Walker, H., ed. *Disappearing Foods* (Totnes 1995)

Young, A., *A Six Monthly Tour through the North of England* (1770)

MANUSCRIPTS FROM THE WORDSWORTH TRUST COLLECTION

Dorothy Wordsworth's commonplace books	DC MS 26 & 120
Fricker Family recipe book	MS E 907
Joanna Hutchinson's recipe book	WLMS Hutchinson 1/8/52
Martha Fricker's recipe book	MS E 907
Mary Wordsworth's recipe book	MS G 2/14/1

NOTES

ABBREVIATIONS

Date only, e.g. 10/1/00, *Dorothy Wordsworth's Journal*
DCMS   manuscript commonplace books of Dorothy Wordsworth
F   manuscript recipe book, Fricker faniily
JH   "   "   "   Joanna Hutchinson
MF   "   "   "   Martha Fricker
MW   "   "   "   Mary Wordsworth
LMW   Letters of Mary Wordsworth
LSH Letters of Sara Hutchinson
LWDW   Letters of William & Dorothy Wordsworth

Chapter 1

THE WORDSWORTHS & THEIR RECIPES

1.   Moorman I 29
2.   Prelude II, 79-85
3.   *ibid.* III 49-52
4.   *ibid.* III 42-45
5.   Moorman I 245
6.   25/7/00,Hart 52,81
7.   7/8/00
8.   28/8/00, 11/12/01, 18/12/01, 13/3/02
9.   LWDW VIII 96
10.   16/10/02, 23/10/02, 8/12/02, 24/12/02, 16/1/03
11.   Moorman I 16
12.   Young IV 59
13.   LWDW I 133
14.   4/10/02
15.   Wordsworth Trust MS 9/90/31
16.   LMW 88 19/9/22
17.   LWDW I 351
18.   Wordsworth Trust WLMS Hutchinson 1/6/52

19.   Holmes 78
20.   *ibid.* 374
21.   *ibid.* 133
22.   LWDW III 11, 42
23.   Wordsworth Trust E 907
24.   Wordsworth Trust E 907
25.   Hart 76

Chapter 2

AT HOME IN GRASMERE

1.   The Waggoner
2.   LWDW I 317
3.   Rawnsley, E.F., 2
4.   Brears (1988) 77
5.   Hudson I 60
6.   24/12/02, LWDW I 622
7.   LWDW I 188
8.   9/12/01, 7/5/02, LWDW II 38
9.   Dove Cottage Guidebook (1970) 10, 9/12/01
10.   Personal Talk
11.   LWDW I 661

12. *ibid.* 622
13. 8/11/00, 7,17 & 18/4/02, 3/7/02
14. 8/11/00, 7,17&18/3/02, 3/7/02, 14/2/02
15. 12&24/11/01, 24/1/02, LWDW I 636
16. 29/5/00, 9,11,13 & 19/6/00, 2/8/00
17. 12/6/00, 19/6/00
18. 10/6/00, 23 & 25/6/00
19. 15 & 22/5/00, 30-31/6/00, 21/8/00
20. 4-5/8/00
21. 9/6/00, 10/9/00
22. Hart 52
23. 9/6/00
24. 11/6/00
25. 9/6/00
26. 16/5/00
27. 16/5/00
28. 15/5/00 to 30/8/00
29. 22/10/00, 14/5/02, De Quincey 260
30. 16/5/00
31. 11/6/00
32. 19/5/00
33. 4-5/6/00
34. Prelude III 528-9, Thompson 106
35. 24/11/01
36. 27/1/02, 27.4.02
37. Christies, London Saleroom, 7/6/1996
38. 5/2/02, 23/2/02
39. LWDW II 205
40. 17/5/02, 16/6/00
41. LWDW II 394
42. 8/2/02, 16/6/00
43. 17/5/00, 30/8/00, 10/10/00, 1/11/02
44. 29/11/01,LWDW III13
45. Coleridge 283
46. Hart 50, 6/3/02, 11/1/03, 30/4/00, 13/1/02, 20/10/00
47. Hart 56
48. LWDW I 476
49. Rawnsley, H.D., 15,23,28,35,36
50. Hart 18
51. 26/5/00. 2/6/00
52. Hurst 52
53. 11/6/02
54. 31/10/02, 21/11/02
55. LWDW I 471
56. *ibid.* I 480-81, II 19, I 275
57. *ibid.* I 480

58. *ibid.* II 31
59. *ibid.* II 207, Moorman II 133
60. 23/11/00, 5/12/00, 22/12/00, 7/12/02, 8/12/02
61. Moorman II 87
62. LWDW I 403, 415, 481
63. *ibid.* II 51
64. Rawnsley, H.D., 35
65. *ibid.* 28
66. 14/3/02
67. Rawnsley, H.D., 14
68. 1/9/00, 22/5/02, 7/3/02, 17-18/3/02, 11/2/02, 4/12/02, LWDW I 636
69. 12/11/01, 22/11/01, 24/11/01, 24/12/02
70. 4/3/02, 12/6/02
71. LSH 202
72. LMW 207, 4/4/38
73. LWDW I 362, 4/3/02
74. De Quincey 127
75. Lee 63
76. De Quincey 127
77. *ibid.* 218
78. National Trust, Cleveland Court, Somerset
79. 7/8/00, LWDW II 453, 13/3/02, 16/1/03
80. 11/1/03, 2/7/00, 7/4/02, 16/5/00, Moorman II 135
81. LWDW I 661, 22/12/02
82. 25/6/00
83. Coleridge to Humphry Davy 25/7/00
84. LWDW I 442
85. *ibid.* I 263
86. LSH 61, 1/8/13
87. *ibid.* I 324, 19/9/26, LWDW III 539
88. 30/12/02, 28/10/00, 28/12/01, Hart 145
89. LWDW I 419
90. Hart 144, LWDW VII 448
91. Coleridge 723
92. 10/12/00, 5/11/01, 29/12/01
93. Moorman I 578
94. LWDW I 419
95. *ibid.* I 440
96. DCMS 26. 143
97. LWDW I 461
98. *ibid.* II 480, 661
99. *ibid.* II 282
100. *ibid.* II 279-81

101. LSH 9, -/10/08
102. MF 26
103. LWDW II 376-8
104. *ibid.* II 282
105. *ibid.* II 407, 491-3
106. *ibid.* II 493, III 15, 38
107. *ibid.* II 114, 519, 554
108. *ibid.* III 86,11, 114
109. *ibid.* III 114, 519, 554
110. LSH 57, 60, 1/8/13
111. LMW 49, 12/1/19
112. LWDW III 140
113. *ibid.* III 554
114. LSH 203, 11/9/20, 206, 19/9/20
115. LWDW III 554
116. Rawnsley, H.D., 12-13

27. 15/8/00, LWDW III 38 26/7/12
28. MW 16
29. MF 23
30. Moorman I 436, LSH 247 9/11/22
31. Coleridge 584
32. *ibid.* 974
33. 3/8/00
34. Dods 188
35. JH 4
36. Wondrausch 229
37. LWDW 508
38. LSH 51 9/3/13, 163 28/10/19
39. *ibid.* 210 19/9/20
40. Raffald 24, Wondrausch 230
41. JH 22
42. Moorman I 24
43. JH 3

Chapter 3
OF MAIN COURSES

1. Nicholson 309
2. Young IV 591
3. LWDW II 205
4. *ibid.* III 50
5. 14/3/02, 7/4/02, Thompson 102, Hart 52
6. LMW 190, 21/9/37
7. Raffald 161
8. MF 32
9. MW 18
10. Coleridge 173
11. JH 2
12. 31/12/01
13. JH 3
14. Coleridge 305-7
15. JH 3
16. LWDW I 357
17. 29/10/00, 11/11/0, 29/11/01
18. Dickinson 201 'Giblet Pie', Dods 387
19. Rundell 133
20. 3/7/02
21. F.12
22. JH 1
23. JH 2
24. 9/12/01, 12/11/01, 24/11/01, 24/1/02, LWDW I 661, 25/12/05
25. JH 2
26. 17/3/02, 22/5/02, 1/9/00

Chapter 4
OF COLD PUDDINGS

1. JH 14
2. F 20
3. F 19
4. F 14
5. MW 20
6. JH 11
7. MW 20
8. MF 22
9. F 15
10. JH 10
11. F 25
12. F 3
13. F 23
14. F 19
15. MW 17
16. Glasse 84
17. JH 12

Chapter 5
OF HOT PUDDINGS & SWEET PIES

1. 29/5/02
2. Private Collection
3. LWDW I 661
4. MF 37

5. 16/5/00
6. Farley 183
7. JH 35
8. 7/6/00
9. Anon. 80
10. Private Collection
11. Raffald 80
12. JH 1
13. 28/12/01
14. 11/1/03
15. MW 17
16. 8/12/01, 25/1/02, 12/6/02, 3/7/02,
     4/3/92, 29/3/02
17. 28/12/01
18. Bradley II 122-3
19. Anon. 57
20. JH 11

Chapter 6

OF BREAD & CAKES

1. 26/1/02
2. Hart 52, 175
3. Hart 81
4. Hart 175
5. JH 27
6. JH 35
7. JH 30
8. F 13
9. MF 37
10. F 16-18
11. F 16-18
12. F 26, Dods 443
13. F 25
14. JH 8
15. Dods 445
16. Dods 446
17. JH 31
18. 13/3/02
19. Raffald 135
20. JH 9
21. Dods 450, Nutt 19
22. JH 9
23. JH 10
24. JH 10
25. F 27
26. Bowness 40

27. 31/5/00, 16/1/03
28. Anon. 74
29. JH 8
30. MF 25
31. F 7
32. JH 34
33. F 6
34. 6/11/00
35. Stead 163
36. White 299
37. F 22
38. JH 1
39. Dove Cottage Guide 116
40. Rawnsley, H.D., 28-9
41. Brears (1991) 85

Chapter 7

OF SWEETS

1. Dickinson 202 Taffy-joinin
2. MF 5
3. MF 8
4. MF 2

Chapter 8

OF PRESERVES & PICKLES

1. JH 14
2. 7/8/00
3. JH 13
4. JH 12
5. JH 34-5
6. MW 20
7. Wilson 52
8. MW 19
9. MF 22
10. JH 13
11. MW 21-2
12. JH 17
13. MF 11
14. JH 5
15. JH 5
16. Nott 202 'To Pick Lemons'
17. Farley 237
18. Farley 236
19. JH 6

20. Nott 203 'To Pickle Walnuts'
21. JH 6

Chapter 9
OF CHEESE & CURDS

1. Dickinson 203 'Milkin ring'
2. *ibid.* 203 'Blown milk'
3. *ibid.* 203 'Cumt milk'
4. *ibid.* 203 'Cheese Rennet'
5. Rollinson 45
6. 10/10/01, 9/11/01
7. 13/2/02, 26/11/01
8. DCMS 143
9. LWDW I 470, 450-4
10. *ibid.* II 58
11. *ibid.* II 282
12. *ibid.* II 453
13. LSH 19, 19/4/09
14. LMW 4, 11/8/13
15. LWDW III 15
16. LMW 20, 11/10/14
17. MF 38
18. MW 9
19. JH 16
20. JH 16
21. JH 16
22. LMW 169, 19/8/37

Chapter 10
OF DRINKS

1. Prelude I 37, 44, 45
2. LWDW I 460
3. 27/4/02, 7/5/02
4. 21/6/02
5. LWDW I 385
6. *ibid.* II 361-2, 23/8/00
7. *ibid.* II 403
8. *ibid.* II 407
9. *ibid.* II 453
10. *ibid.* III 82,85,94
11. 7/5/02, 23/11/00, 1/8/00, 25/6/00
12. 25/10/01, 10/11/01
13. 26/10/01, 27-8/1/02, 28/10/00
14. Dickinson 75

15. 4-5/11/02
16. Coleridge 1300, ?/12/00
17. JH 15
18. MW 18
19. LMW 362, 28/4/28
20. F 9
21. JH 27
22. 2/1/03
23. LWDW I 317, 475-6
24. *ibid.* 466, 480
25. *ibid.* 494
26. F 10
27. JH 28
28. MW 10
29. LWDW I 317, Hart 207
30. *ibid.* III 140
31. Coleridge 164
32. LMW 127, 16/7/ 28
33. LWDW III 409
34. LMW 202, 11/9/20
35. MW 11
36. JH 23
37. JH 15
38. JH 20
39. JH 20
40. JH 19
41. JH 24
42. JH 37
43. JH 19
44. JH 23
45. F 1
46. 5/10/02
47. based on a number of contemporary recipes
48. 48 4/5/02
49. 49 1/9/00
50. 50 JH 15
51. 22/4/02
52. F 10

Chapter 11
OF PACE EGGS

1. Sullivan 164
2. Hone I 426-8, II 450
3. Moorman II 430, 602, 611,

Rawnsley, H.D., 31
4.   LSH 350, 7/11/30
5.   *ibid.* 175, 19/11/29, 177, 25/11/29
6.   e.g. Newall 284-5 & colour plate XVIII
7.   Information from R.Miller
8.   Lady Richardson in Wordsworth,
      C., II 446-7
9.   Hone, op. cit.
10. Sullivan 164
11. Newall op. cit. 336,339, Thompson 34
12. Hone, II 450

33. JH 25
34. MF 4
35. JH 29
36. JH 34
37. 24-5/6/02
38. JH 25
39. MW 12
40. DCMS 26 143

Chapter 12

OF HOME REMEDIES

1.   MW 8
2.   MF 8
3.   MW 15
4.   MW 15
5.   JH 31
6.   MF 9
7.   24/11/00
8.   21/4/02, 4-5/11/00
9.   8/2/02
10. DCMS 26 142
11. JH 33
12. JH 33
13. JH 33
14. JH 33
15. DCMS 120
16. JH 32
17. JH 32
18. DMS 26 142
19. MW 14
20. JH 7
21. JH 18
22. 10/10/00
23. JH 33
24. OED 204 'Cold Cream'
25. JH 29
26. 19/3/02
27. 4/10/00, 11/11/01
28. e.g. LWDW I 505, III 131
29. *ibid.* VIII 236
30. MW 8
31. MW 13
32. JH 7

GENERAL INDEX

A

Ale Mearnce 166
Allan Bank 19, 44, 48, 50–51, 53, 152, 189
Ambleside 20, 36, 161, 179, 188
Ashburner
    Peggy 37
    Thomas 40

B

Baldock 47
balls 51
Baty (Bateman), Frank 151
Beaumont
    Lady 36, 41, 165
    Sir George 165
    bees 20, 37. *see also* honey
    hives 38
Beetham's Churn 152
Bill, Mary. *See* Cooks
Bird, Richard 20
Birkett, Richard 177
Bishop Middleton 25
blackening 191
Blacklock, W.J. 38
Bouth 39
Bradley, Richard 102
Bristol 28–30, 81, 142
Burnett, George 29

C

Cambridge 20, 24, 33, 37, 102
Carr, Mr 23
Charlton, Mrs 144
christening 49
Christmas 36, 42, 45, 47, 49, 51, 70, 96,
101–102, 166–167
Churn, Taylor's 152

Clarkson, Catherine 57, 152
Clary 170
    Clary Wine 170
coal 23, 34, 39–40, 42, 107
Cockermouth 9, 19–21, 188
Cockyn family 161
Coleorton 44
Coleridge
    family 37, 42, 47
    Hartley 29
    Samuel Taylor 7–8, 13–14, 28–29, 34,
        40, 42, 44–45, 47, 60, 62–63, 70,
        101, 107, 197
    Sara 30
Colwith 39
Cooks
    Bill, Mary 53
    cooks 53
    Dawson, Mary 43, 52–53, 153
    Jane 53
    Mary Anne 53, 74
Cookson
    grandparents 22, 24
    Mr 22, 24
    William 22
Cooper, Margaret 195
Crosthwaite Museum 51
Crump, Mr 48

D

Danvers, Mrs 167
Dawson, Mary. *see* Cooks
De Quincey
    Thomas 46, 197, 200
Dixon, James 178–180
Dockray, Jenny 151
Dove and Olive Bough 22, 33, 35
Dove Cottage 7–9, 13–14, 19, 22, 23, 25,
        28–30, 33, 37–42, 44–46, 49,

52–53, 57, 64, 71, 102, 107, 109,
144, 151–152, 159, 161, 165–166,
172, 178, 184, 188, 189, 191, 193,
195, 197, 199, 202
Dunmail Raise 101, 127–128, 189

E

Easedale 39, 43, 48, 57, 151, 172

F

Fenwick, Miss Isabella 179
Fisher
    John 36, 38, 42–43, 159
    Molly 22, 36, 42–43, 50, 107, 109, 120,152
fishing 7, 36, 73, 161
floor 21, 34–36, 51–52
    chalked 51
Fricker
    Edith 8, 28–29
    family 8, 13, 28, 30, 133, 165, 170
    Martha 13, 28–30, 50, 53, 59, 86, 88,
        96, 111, 122, 153, 184, 193,
        198–199
    Mary 28–29
    Sara 8, 28–30
fuel 34, 38, 48, 53, 99, 112

G

Gallow Hill 25, 63, 152, 192
Grasmere 5, 7–9, 13, 19–20, 22–23, 25, 28,
        33–34, 36, 39, 41, 43–44, 47–49,
        51, 53, 57, 107, 127–128, 153, 159,
        161, 165, 179, 195, 197, 199
    Church 49
    Rectory 19, 51, 153
Grassy Nook 153
Green
    George 39
    Sally 43
    Sarah 39
Greta Hall 29, 30, 47, 49, 197
Grey, Barbara 119–120

H

Halifax 20–22, 41, 125

Hawkshead 19, 37, 39, 75, 198
High Bakestones 127
High Broadrain 161
Hindwell 28, 152, 153
Hollins, The 161
Hugessen, Mrs 184
Hutchinson
    family 23, 28
    George 23, 25
    Henry 23, 25, 73
    Joanna 8, 13, 15, 19, 23, 25–28, 30, 44,
        53, 60–62, 66–67, 69, 72–73,
        76–77, 81, 87, 98, 108, 117, 121,
        126, 140, 143, 146, 154, 162,
        164, 168, 184–185, 188–190,
        193, 198–199
    John 195
    Mary 7, 24
    Sara 2, 13, 19, 23, 43–44, 48, 50–53,
        63, 73, 107–108, 128, 199
    Thomas 23, 24, 70

I

Ibbotson family 161
Ingleton 40

J

Jackson
    Jim 159
    Mr 51, 159

K

Kendal 20, 23, 39, 40, 57, 98, 119–120,
    161, 180, 197–198
Keswick 8, 20, 29, 30, 37, 40, 51, 53, 101,
    151, 161, 165, 189
King
    Mrs 108–109, 170
    Mr Thomas 169
King's Head 49, 101–102, 151, 161, 165
Kirk Ulpha 49
kitchen 20–21, 34–36, 40, 43, 50–51, 53,
    57–58, 63, 68, 70, 83, 107, 127,
    154, 161

FOOD & RECIPE INDEX

HOUSEHOLD & REMEDIES INDEX

Excellent Press
Ludlow

OTHER EXCELLENT PRESS PUBLICATIONS

Traditional Food in Shropshire

by Peter Brears

In Shropshire, the largest and most fertile of England's inland counties, the quality of locally-produced food is second to none. This book, the first major study of the subject, draws on the widest range of local evidence to show how kitchens were designed and equipped, and various foods cooked, in cottages, halls and baker's shops, either for everyday meals, or for special celebrations. There are also over a hundred traditional Shropshire recipes, each having been cooked in order to present them in modern form for anyone wishing to accurately re-create them today, including the histories and method for those great local specialities, the Shrewsbury Cake and the Shrewsbury Simnel.

Illustrated with many colour plates and line drawings by the author.

ISBN 1 900318 39 3   216pp   £19.95

Excellent Press
Ludlow

Reminiscences of an Old West Country Clergyman

by W.H.Thornton

Privately printed on the author's retirement in 1897 and recently rediscovered, this is a classic account of country life in Exmoor and Dartmoor during the Victorian period. Mr Thornton was a hard-riding outdoorsman whose clerical duties and love of the chase brought him into close contact with Devonshire characters of every stripe, from the squire and the bishop to the poorest cottagers, smugglers, thieves and murderers. The feats of riding and long distance walking described will amaze modern readers. Packed full of colourful stories, brilliantly told.

ISBN 1 900318 38 5   240pp in soft covers   £12.99

Excellent Press
Ludlow

LUDLOW FOOD SERIES

A popular series of delicious pocket books in hardcover from Shropshire's home of good food and local produce.

A Sausage Book

by Helen Saberi

A feast of sausages, from Cumberland traditional to Pigs in Blankets and Dublin Coddle, by this well known food writer.

ISBN 1 900318 31 8   60pp   £6.99

A Pudding Book

by Helen Saberi

All kinds of puddings are featured, including Apple Brown Betty, Poor Knights of Windsor, Drowned Baby, Sticky Toffee and Chocolate with pears and brandy. No concessions are made to calorie-watchers.

ISBN 1 900318 30 X   60pp   £6.99

Excellent Press
Ludlow

Good Cookery from Wales

by Lady Llanover

Anyone interested in British cookery will be fascinated by this selection from her famous book of 1867 containing some of the best traditional Welsh dishes. Lady Llanover was a famous hostess and cultural pioneer in Wales. Her cookery shows a sensitive appreciation of local produce in her descriptions of classic, but simple Welsh fare, like oatbreads and toasted cheese, along with the occasional grander dishes, such as Salt Duck and Chicken & Leek pie.

ISBN 1 900318 32 6   60pp   £6.99

Ginger bread

1/2 tt Treacle 1/2 tt Sugar 9 oz Butter
Ginger to your taste — a few cloves & a
little lemon skin — Rub the butter &
as much flour as will make the pay
stiff adding flour till it is so when
you knead it — when the butter &
treacle are stiff with cold set them
within the air of the fire to soften
in warm weather this is not
necessary —

Blacking

4 oz Ivory black 2 oz Coarse sug.
mixed well with a quart of vi-
gar — add carefully 1/2 oz Oil of
vitriol stirring very well w
a stick in a deep earthenware vesse
last of all add two large spoons
of sweet oil —

To preserve fruit of any ki
Gather the fruit when dry & to
a pint of fruit take 1/4 tt loaf
Sugar (or fine soft will do) — put
the fruit & Sugar into jars o